Praise for
When God Says "Go"

"Few books have stilled my soul and shifted my faith perspective like *When God Says 'Go'*. Elizabeth's vast knowledge of scripture, her invitation to explore the stories of biblical men and women, and her encouragement to saturate ourselves in truth rather than circumstance is powerfully transformative. If you're looking for a deep dive into the reminder that God is always with you, *When God Says 'Go'* will be your new favorite resource and study guide."

–Bekah Jane Pogue, author of *Choosing REAL*,
national speaker, writing & speaking coach,
Encouraging Soul Care at bekahpogue.com

"Elizabeth Laing Thompson holds your hand, dismisses your excuses, gives you fuel for the race, and empowers you to take that first walk on the waves in *When God Says 'Go'*. Be inspired by her authentic, friendly voice and her biblical arsenal. You're not alone. She has stood where you stand, and she jumped. This book of faith will help you jump too."

–Andy Lee, author of *A Mary Like Me: Flawed Yet Called* and
*The Book of Ruth Key Word Bible Study:
A 31-Day Journey to Hope and Promise*

"*When God Says 'Go'* offered poignant and heartfelt reminders about our unique opportunities to serve God and how to peacefully trust His ways. Elizabeth's beautifully told stories reignited my heart and commitment for going all in for Jesus. Whether it requires a huge transformation or a 'yes' right where we are, giving God our all is truly the best way to live. This book will challenge you, convict you, make you chuckle, and leave you wiping tears before you close the last page."

–Courtney Westlake, author of *A Different Beautiful*

"If you are hesitant about what God has called you to do, *When God Says 'Go'* is a must-read book that will transform your fear into courage. Elizabeth Laing Thompson breaks down biblical examples of scripture in a way that will leave you wanting to read more. This book will encourage you to boldly answer God's call on your life with confidence and expectation—to courageously say yes when God says go."

–Caroline Harries, author of *In Due Time*, blogger

"*When God Says 'Go'* gives us the gentle nudge and the affirmed push to step into who God is calling us to be. Elizabeth explains that road may not always be easy, but neither has it been easy for anyone God has drawn into a meaningful calling. I'm so grateful for Elizabeth's words, for the way she both encourages us to be bold and nourishes our hearts with her writing. I highly recommend this book for any woman looking down the individually incredible path God has set for each of us."

–Emily Ley, author of *A Simplified Life*

"Elizabeth is an absolute marvel. She writes in a style that is witty, relatable, and downright fun to read. In *When God Says 'Go,'* Elizabeth bridges time and helps us connect with biblical characters from long ago. They become contemporary friends instead of ancient acquaintances. We feel as if we are right there with them as they wrestle with feelings of fear, unease, and confusion while listening to God's call of, *Go!* This book is a must-read for anyone not quite certain of how to proceed when God calls us forward. Isn't that all of us? As Elizabeth says, 'God is calling us all to go somewhere new in our walk with Him.' I am so relieved that Elizabeth helps and encourages us to rise to the challenge. She is our trusty trail-guide whose wisdom we are all fortunate to heed."

–Sarah Philpott, author of *Loved Baby: 31 Devotions Helping You Grieve and Cherish Your Child after Pregnancy Loss*

When God Says *go*

Rising to challenge and change
without losing your *confidence*,
your *courage*, or your *cool*

Elizabeth Laing Thompson

SHILOH RUN PRESS
An Imprint of Barbour Publishing, Inc.

Print ISBN 978-1-68322-555-3

eBook Editions:
Adobe Digital Edition (.epub) 978-1-68322-570-6
Kindle and MobiPocket Edition (.prc) 978-1-68322-571-3

Cover Design: Faceout Studio, www.faceoutstudio.com

Published by Shiloh Run Press, an imprint of Barbour Publishing, Inc., 1810 Barbour Drive, Uhrichsville, Ohio 44683, www.shilohrunpress.com.

Our mission is to inspire the world with the life-changing message of the Bible.

ecpa Member of the
Evangelical Christian
Publishers Association

Printed in the United States of America.

Dedication

For my courageous in-laws, Bill and Glenda Thompson, who have never said no when God said go. How grateful I am that He finally said, "Go live two miles away from Kevin and Elizabeth."

Acknowledgments

An author's name stands alone on the front of a book, but the truth is, a book is a team effort.

I am still awed that God is letting me do this writing thing. After so many years working and waiting, so many years thinking He was saying no, I'm still getting used to Him saying, "Go." Every morning I wake up and think, *Really, Lord? You want me to write for You today?* How I love doing this for Him—and with Him. I am deeply thankful for the astounding privilege.

Now for the people. . .First (always) my husband, Kevin. He didn't know he was signing on to be a writer spouse when we said, "I do" (in my defense, I didn't know either), but he has generously and joyfully embraced the role; in fact, he should give Awesome Writer Husband lessons. Last year when I said, "Hey, remember that time we had two babies in fourteen months? Can we do that again. . .only this time with books?"—he didn't blink, just said, "Who needs sleep anyway?" He kept our family running and kept me sane. When I got home from writing marathons, he nodded and smiled at my hyper-caffeinated, near-manic babblings and pretended they made sense, and (perhaps best of all) he had the kitchen clean and the dishwasher running. I'm forever-and-always thankful that God lets me go through life at your side.

Thank you to Cassidy, Blake, Avery, and Sawyer for the snuggle hugs, the snort laughs, and the silly games. Being your mom is my favorite thing.

This book would not exist without my in-laws, Bill and Glenda

Thompson. Not only has their inspiring example taught me how to follow God wherever He leads, but they also stepped in to help our crazy life keep running full-steam-ahead while I wrote. They chauffeured, they invited my kids to the Thompson Restaurant, they pulled piano lesson duty—for all this (and so much more), thank you.

I am grateful to my parents and siblings and siblings-in-law for their constant encouragement and faithful prayers. I have watched my parents go for God their entire lives—their courage, constancy, and perseverance have taught me (and many others) what it means to follow God at every stage of life. My effervescent mother asked for daily updates and responded with breathless enthusiasm every time, as only a mother would care to do. My sister Alexandra provided approximately 5,000 confidence boosts when insecurity struck—thank you for always wearing rose-colored glasses with me.

My sister-in-law Talia was a life-saver in the final weeks of writing. She took time away from her own intense graduate work and mom life to help me research. She read the sections that most intimidated me to write, and her insights made them better. She is not only brilliant, but also humble, generous, and kind.

My brother-in-law Byron made the book trailer—he has the gift of finding the soul of a project and capturing it on screen.

I'd be lost without my writing partner, Emma—*parabatai*, first reader, forever friend. She read the whole book several times through and performed her usual (and yet oh-so-unusual-because-she-is-oh-so-gifted) magic. As Jonathan did for David at Horesh, she helped me find strength in God (1 Samuel 23:16).

My agent, Jessica Kirkland, is a rock-solid source of encouragement and guidance in life, in faith, and in writing. She pointed me toward this topic (ahem, thank you for the title!), helped me work through a tricky chapter that had me stumped, and helped me better grasp this book's message.

I am delighted to be working with the team at Barbour. They are excellent in their work, God-centered in their lives, and patient with my many questions. Kelly McIntosh is ever gracious, with an email-return speed that is almost supernatural. The marketing team is creative, persistent, and positive. Shalyn Sattler makes the challenge of marketing feel like an adventure, not a burden. Liesl Davenport sweetly pretends my dumb questions aren't dumb, and she always goes the extra mile. Lauren Schneider did a beautiful job copyediting, knowing where to correct and where to let me blur the lines between adjectives and adverbs. Many thanks to Ashley Schrock for another wonderful book cover—it's perfect! Thank you to Mary Burns, marketing guru; Faith Nordine, proofreading ninja; and Morgan Dreher, typesetter extraordinaire.

Thank you to all the friends and family who so generously allowed me to share your stories in this book. I am humbled and honored that you entrusted precious pieces of your life to me so that others might be encouraged and inspired.

Thank you to my church for praying with and for me as I wrote. Thank you for looking past my ball caps and crazy eyes at midweek. It is a joy to serve God and our city together.

Thank you to writer friends old and new—Jeanie, Katie, Lara, Tracy, Bekah, Andy, Emily, Muriel, Gail, Susan—for all the encouragement and companionship you have given!

This book was fueled by caffeine brewed by the amazing baristas at my Starbucks (thank you for letting me hog the window seat), and by musical inspiration from The Tenors, George Winston, and Pentatonix.

And to all of you who read this book, thank you. You are on my heart and in my prayers, and I treasure every email and letter you send my way. I pray these words help you find—and embrace—God's call wherever it leads.

Contents

Introduction
When God Says "Go"

*G*o: the smallest of words, the biggest of meanings. It may be one of God's favorite words.

Sometimes life is calm. Secure. Peaceful. Nothing scary, each day much like the one before. That's usually when God shows up. That's usually when God says, "Go."

Sometimes God calls dramatically, in miracle and flame. Sometimes He calls subtly, in stillness and whisper, so soft we won't hear if we aren't listening. Sometimes through His Word, sometimes through a friend, sometimes through life events.

However He speaks, God calls to us all. We are called for different roles, in different ways, at different points in our lives: one season holds one purpose, the next holds another. We are God's people, His instruments, and He wants to use us. As Romans 8:28 puts it, "We know that in all things God works for the good of those who love him, who have been called according to his purpose." *According to His purpose.* God has plans for each of us. He has work for us to do, work He prepared a long time ago, work He has equipped us to accomplish: "For we are God's handiwork, created in Christ Jesus to do good works, which God prepared in advance for us to do" (Ephesians 2:10).

God is calling. . . . Will we answer His call?

1
When God's Call Scares You to Death

Moses' Story

Based on Exodus 3–4

So now go. I am sending *you* to Pharaoh to bring my people out of Egypt."

Moses gapes at the fiery bush, reeling. He shrinks from the light, recoils from the heat, resists the words.

Go.

You.

Egypt.

Go to Egypt, the land of Moses' childhood, the land he fled forty years earlier—and for good reason. Go to Pharaoh, the king who would gladly remove Moses' head from his body without thinking twice.

Moses bows low, tries to find respectful words to speak back to the God in the bush. "Who am I that I should go to Pharaoh?"

"I will be with you. . ."

As the voice goes on, Moses sits back on his heels. He wants to say, "I have no doubt You are more than qualified to confront Pharaoh—but me? Why *me*? Are You sure You have called the right man?"

Forty years ago, maybe young Moses would have risked a return trip to Egypt, even embraced the challenge—bold Moses, confident Moses, defender-of-the-Hebrews Moses. Unmarried Moses, childless Moses, adoptive-son-of-the-princess Moses, who could afford the luxury of courage. Moses who once was brave enough to challenge an Egyptian overseer.

Maybe this flaming God has missed the last four decades Moses has spent away from Egypt, hiding in Midian: safe years, happy years—raising kids, tending sheep. Moses tries to picture leading the sheep home this evening, telling his wife, Zipporah, "So I spoke to a fire in a bush in the woods today—turns out the bush was actually God—or maybe it was the fire that was God, not the bush—anyway, God is sending me back to Egypt to confront Pharaoh and set all his slaves free! I could get killed, but—well, the fire in the bush said I should do it." If he weren't so terrified, it might be almost funny.

But the fire God is waiting for an answer. Moses swallows his objections and plays along, stalling for time. "So, uh, suppose I go to Egypt—which god do I say You are? The Egyptians have never heard of You—a thousand apologies, I mean no offense."

"I AM WHO I AM."

As God explains, orange flames flickering in time to His words, Moses tries to listen, but he can hardly hear past the thundering of his own heart, the objections clamoring for attention.

When God finishes speaking, Moses turns on his logical voice, the one he uses with his children when they get irrational. He has to help this God acknowledge the weakness in the plan—namely, Moses.

"I'm just a nobody Hebrew—an outcast. Maybe there was a time they might have heard me out, but not anymore. What if they don't believe me?"

The bush glows brighter, hotter. "What is that in your hand?"

"A staff."

"Throw it on the ground."

Feeling a little foolish, Moses throws the staff down in front of the bush. The instant the wood hits dirt, it begins to writhe. Moses blinks hard, not trusting his eyes. The staff softens and coils, snakelike—no, wait—it *is* a snake! Golden and glistening in the firelight, its beady yellow eyes fixed on Moses. And now it's rushing toward him, charging.

With a yell, Moses runs, bare feet scrabbling on rocky soil. He trips, falls back onto his elbows, crab-walks backward as fast as he can scramble. The snake follows, slower now, pink tongue flickering, staring Moses down with those hard yellow eyes.

The voice in the bush rumbles—is it *laughing*?—and commands, "Reach out your hand and take the snake by the tail."

The snake has frozen in place at the sound of the voice. Head raised, tongue fluttering, eyes unblinking.

Moses leaps to his feet.

"What are you waiting for?" booms the voice. "Pick up the snake!"

So this is it. Moses has asked too many questions. Shown too much fear. The fire God is going to smite him right here: death by snakebite. At least death will come swiftly—a few hours' agony at most.

Moses reaches a shaking hand toward the snake. It holds still, watching him, as if preparing to strike.

Breathing good-bye to his wife, Moses moves fast. He clamps his fist around the smooth, twitching flesh. Squeezes his eyes shut, waiting for the bite, the burn.

Nothing happens.

He slits one eye open. Shouts in surprise, loses his grip. His staff clatters to the ground. His *staff*. The snake has become a staff again. Slowly Moses bends to pick it up, trembling all over, half laughing with relief.

"That—that was a good trick," he tells the bush. "You got me."

"It is no trick," says the bush. "It will prove to Pharaoh that I am with you."

The voice shows him another marvel, covering Moses' hand in leprosy, healing it again—and at the end of it, Moses' skin is fine, but his head is pounding. He just wants to go home. Home to Zipporah and the family. Home where staffs remain staffs, hands remain leprosy-free, and heads remain firmly attached to bodies.

Perhaps he needs to make his objections more detailed. "Pardon Your servant, Lord. I have never been eloquent. I am slow of speech and tongue." As if to prove his point, Moses' tongue hitches, and he stutters. "These miracles are astounding. But I can't do them justice."

Angry flames roar, stretching high as treetops. Moses cringes away from the billowing heat. Presses tentative fingertips to his face to see if his eyebrows are singed.

The voice growls, "Who gave human beings their mouths? Who makes them deaf or mute? Who gives them sight or makes them blind? Is it not I, the Lord? Now go; I will help you speak and will teach you what to say."

Moses buries his face in his hands, exhausted. This voice, this God, is relentless. Moses can't hint or hedge anymore; he will just have to say it. "Pardon Your servant, Lord—I am honored by Your request, Your faith in me—but please. Please send someone else."

Flames surge; heat washes over him in a wave. He tries to run but there's nowhere to go.

❦

Poor Moses. He thought he had left Egypt and danger behind forty years ago. Gone was the bold young man, the cocky prince of Egypt who thought he could save people. Make a difference.

No, Moses knew better now. Life had taught him different. His place was here now: here in Midian, far from Egypt; here with his wife, their family, his sheep. It wasn't a thrilling life, but it was safe. Comfortable. Predictable.

And then a fiery bush starts talking. And this is no idle chatter—weather predictions, sheep-shearing strategies—no, the bush has plans. *I AM* has plans.

"So now go. I am sending you."

Back to Egypt, to danger, to an unpredictable life with dizzying purpose.

When God Changes Your Plans

I am thirty-three, and life has never been better. Happy marriage, three crazy kids, fixer-upper house in a great neighborhood. My parents and in-laws both live nearby (translation: endless supply of free babysitting), I have finally found close friends, we love our church. After eight years, this town has become home. I'm ready to mark out a burial plot in the woods behind our house, because I never want even my bones to leave this place. A few months later, God says, "Move."

I'm like, "Excuse me? You didn't—You don't mean *me*?"

And He says, "Go sell your house, leave your extended family, and move. Go to a city where you've never lived and know not one single soul, and start a new church with your husband, your kids, and a handful of strangers."

I fill our boxes with tears.

∽

I'm sitting in a history class in college, listening to this girl laugh in one breath about drinking beer out of her rugby boot then rant in the next breath about how she's fed up with hypocrisy in Christianity. I'm insecure, reserved; she's intimidating, outspoken. But as class ends the Holy Spirit whispers, "Give." The girl sprints out of class. I shoulder my bag and sprint after her, waving an invitation to a Bible study.

∽

I'm stuck. I've been stuck for a while. People hurt me—worse, they hurt people I love—and I retreated. Built an invisible box around my heart and locked myself inside where it's safe. There is no risk-taking inside this box. No conflict, no potential for disappointment or betrayal. For months, years, I ignore the knock at the door. I keep my box clean, love and serve Jesus as hard as I can from inside these walls, my fortress. But the knocking is becoming louder. Insistent. Deafening. I press my ear against the door, already knowing what I will hear. God's voice, kind but firm, speaks gentle through the keyhole: "Grow." With shaking hands and wounded heart, I fumble for the key.

God Is Always Calling

Our God is always calling His people to go: to move, to give, to grow. Moses, Abigail, Mary, Jeremiah. . . God called them all to fulfill His purposes, just as He calls us today. Our Bible heroes responded much as we do: with a jumbled-up inner storm of excitement and fear, insecurity and hope. Like us, they faced doubt, regret, weakness. Their stories and struggles can help us face our own.

The question isn't *Is God calling?*, because God is always calling. Always urging us onward, giving us purpose, encouraging us to grow. The question is *Will we answer His call?*

Maybe it's time to go. Go somewhere new, someplace we've never been. A geographical place, a spiritual place, a relational place. Maybe it's time to move forward after being stuck with one foot in the past. Or time to go deeper—in Bible study or intimacy. Time to go higher—in prayer or in dreams.

Maybe it's time to give: to use talents and opportunities God has given.

Or maybe it's time to grow, right where we are: to dig into the Word, dive into our heart, and become the person God is calling us to be.

When God says, "Go," we face a choice. Will we swallow hard and step up, saying, "Here am I. Send me!" (Isaiah 6:8)? Or will we sit back and stay safe, stammering, "But Lord. . ."?

Whether we're ready or not, God is calling us all to go somewhere new in our walk with Him. So what are we waiting for? Let's answer His call. Let's go for it.

Let's Go Deeper. . .

For Further Study
Read about Moses' early adult life in Exodus 2:11–25. What signs of courage and leadership do you see, and why do you think Moses lost these traits?

Journal Prompt
1. What specific challenges and changes are you facing right now?
2. What are you most afraid of as you face those challenges?
3. Which call feels the most relevant to your life right now: *move* (move somewhere new, redirect your life in some way), *give* (give more to God or to people), or *grow* (face a weakness, develop a new strength)?

Prayer Prompt
The LORD is my light and my salvation—
  whom shall I fear?
The LORD is the stronghold of my life—
  of whom shall I be afraid? . . .
I remain confident of this:
  I will see the goodness of the LORD
  in the land of the living.
Wait for the LORD;
  be strong and take heart
  and wait for the LORD.
PSALM 27:1, 13–14

2
When It's Not about You

Jeremiah's Story

Based on Jeremiah 1 and 20:9

*J*eremiah.

Something whispers him awake. His eyes spring open to darkness.

Was he dreaming? Sleep cobwebs his thoughts.

He lies still in bed, listening, but all he hears is soft breathing, a few gentle snores from a houseful of sleeping souls, the people he loves most, all crammed into one small home—his brother Nathan's family: wife Leah and children, too many children to count, as Jeremiah likes to tease.

He must have imagined it, the voice.

The cobwebs are thinning, his thoughts clearing. If he wants time alone (and he always wants time alone), he must steal it now.

He eases out of bed, tiptoeing with excruciating care past the children's pallets—one false move and the whole house will wake, clamoring for food, for help, for shoulder rides. Little Joel mumbles in his sleep, and Jeremiah freezes midstep.

He counts to one hundred—the house remains silent but for the sound of Joel sucking his thumb—before deciding it's safe to move. From the peg beside the door he grabs his cloak then opens the door so slowly he's sure he has reached age twenty by the time it opens.

Outside he slips his feet into sandals, breathes deep, and smiles. His favorite hour. The predawn world is strangely hushed, as if even the animals and birds hold their breath, awaiting the sun, awaiting His call.

He considers lighting the lantern he keeps beside the front door for these late-night-early-morning excursions, but decides no, he wants the dark. The privacy, the quiet. He likes to tread lightly, leave no mark, not disturb. Light or no light, he knows the way.

Careful and quiet, by faint moonlight he picks his way to the path that leads to the stream, the path his brother's family walks a dozen times each day fetching water. Come dawn this path will be bustling with women and children bearing buckets.

He steers away from the main path and follows a less-worn route—the animals' path—to a hidden curve where the stream pools beneath a copse of trees. Here the stream slips quietly over stones, a quiet song. His song. The rhythm to his prayers. As he enters the copse and his ears catch the first notes, his heart gives a happy leap, his soul starts to sing: *As the deer pants for streams of water, so my soul pants. . . . When can I go and meet with God?*

The water is black, tipped silver with moonlight. Jeremiah slips off his sandals and steps into the shallows, giving a sharp gasp as the cold bites his ankles. The chill wakes his senses. Jeremiah lifts his hands and begins to pray, mouthing words at first, then building to a quiet murmur. It's too early for shouting.

As night's black softens to navy, Jeremiah returns to the bank. From a notch in a tree he pulls down an old blanket and lays it folded on the ground. He kneels.

He is in between psalms, just listening—the lullaby the water sings to the banks, the tales the wind tells to the trees, the *scritch-scritch* of waking animals scurrying in the underbrush—when suddenly it all falls silent. So silent he is sure he can hear the heartbeat of the earth. And in the nothing, a quiet voice calls.

"Jeremiah."

He is so startled, he leaps to his feet. His eyes search the trees—dark shadows with reaching arms. Mist creeps along the ground. "N–Nathan?"

Louder now, and closer: "Jeremiah."

In the voice is the thrum of the ocean, the roar of the lion, the call of the wind.

Overwhelmed, Jeremiah feels his eyes fill and his throat seal.

He covers his ears, and this time he hears the voice as if from within his own soul. Gentler now—the music of the stream, *his* stream, familiar strains now given shape. Lyrics.

"Before I formed you in the womb I knew you."

Jeremiah falls to his knees, claws at his feet to remove his shoes on this holy ground—*Oh yes, already barefoot.* His mind is frantic, splintered thoughts sprinting. *What have I done—oh, help, what do I—?* He can't complete a thought.

Again comes the voice, soft as water: "Before you were born I set you apart. I appointed you a prophet to the nations."

Jeremiah is shocked into speech. He has begun training to be a priest, but—a *prophet*? One who hears from God and *speaks for* God? Jeremiah's heart pounds out a painful rhythm. "Ah, Lord God! I do not know how to speak. I am too—"

Too what? His mind offers a dozen deprecations, all true: *immature, inexperienced, shy.*

At last he settles on a word: "I am too young." He bites back the rest of what he wants to say, sure the Lord won't appreciate the sarcasm: *Just ask the other priests at Anathoth—they won't even let me near the incense for fear I'll burn the place down.*

The voice takes on a stern edge—it sounds remarkably like Jeremiah's father, Hilkiah, rest his soul. "Do not say, 'I am only a child.'"

Jeremiah bows low and nods vigorously, his forehead scraping against the rough grain of the woolen blanket. In the silence, he anticipates the Lord's next lines, the words he has always needed to hear, has secretly longed to hear. The words he imagines his father would say were he still living: *"You are chosen for a reason, my son. Your gifts. . .your heart. . .your training. It's why we named you Jeremiah, 'May Jehovah exalt.'"*

But no. The voice says, "You will go to everyone I send you to, and whatever I command you, you shall speak."

Jeremiah's panicked thoughts skip to Samuel the prophet, his hero. Samuel spoke for God. He judged the nation. Appointed Saul king, then prophesied his demise. Appointed David. A fluttering starts in Jeremiah's gut. He really might be ill all over his mat.

Surely Jeremiah wouldn't be *that* kind of prophet.... Maybe he'd just be the sit-humbly-at-the-temple-circumcising-babies-and-comforting-local-widows-and-occasionally-forecasting-minor-droughts kind of prophet. Surely there were no big proclamations with national significance in his future. No appointments with kings.

He pictures meeting King Josiah. Tries to imagine himself walking down marbled hallways, sitting at long tables with important rulers from Egypt and Babylon. Fear closes a fist around his throat; he fights for breath.

As if reading his thoughts, the voice declares, "Do not be afraid of them, for I am with you and will rescue you."

A cold wind blows, and Jeremiah finds himself on his feet, upright, unsure how he got there. Fog curls around his ankles, his legs. The sky has lightened to gray.

Jeremiah's lips tingle and warm. He presses his fingers against them. His mouth fills with a sweetness—berries and honey and wine. It chases back the fear in his throat. Bewildered and delighted, he almost laughs.

The voice sounds almost amused. "See, I have put My words in your mouth."

The warmth is spreading down his throat, flooding his veins.

"See, today I appoint you over nations and kingdoms to uproot and tear down, to destroy and overthrow, to build and to plant."

He sees visions—an almond tree, a boiling pot—and trembles at their meaning. The fire fills his bones.

At last the Lord says, "Get yourself ready! Stand up and say to them whatever I command you. Do not be terrified by them, or

I will terrify you before them. Today I have made you a fortified city, an iron pillar and a bronze wall to stand against the whole land—against the kings of Judah, its officials, its priests, and the people of the land."

With every word from the Lord, the warmth within grows hotter, ever hotter. The Lord's voice strengthens until Jeremiah feels the words thrum inside him, changing the rhythm of his heart. "They will fight against you but will not overcome you, for I am with you and will rescue you."

In the east, the sun crowns the horizon, an explosion of light and flame—and Jeremiah watches the fireball rise, finally knowing what it is to burn.

∞

"Ah, Lord, I am too young."

Too young. Too old. Too weak. Too wounded. Too fearful. Too selfish. Too. . .me.

Ever felt that way when you felt God pushing you forward? Ever wanted to list all the reasons why you're the wrong person for the job? Turns out you're in good company. And not just with little people like me; you're in good company with great people in the Bible! The Bible gives us a number of stories where God calls people to new roles they weren't expecting—and didn't really want. Their responses—sometimes heroic, sometimes humorous—reflect our own. Like us they stammered. Like us they panicked. Like us they begged for a way out—*any way out*.

Ready for a fun Bible study? Let's take a look at what some of our spiritual ancestors said and did when God called them.

First Jeremiah, whom we've just met: "Ah, Lord, I do not know how to speak. I am too young!" (Jeremiah 1:6 NIV 1984).

Then Gideon, commissioned by an angel to fight an impossible war: "But Lord, how can I rescue Israel? My clan is the weakest in the whole tribe of Manasseh, and I am the least in my entire family!" (Judges 6:15 NIV 1984).

Last Moses, who had more excuses than the others put together: "Who am I that I should go? . . . What if they do not believe me or listen to me? . . . I am slow of speech and tongue. . . . Please send someone else!"

Are you chuckling yet? Just a little? And do you see a pattern? All these people responded to God's call in the same way—*by looking to themselves*. They basically said to God, "Excuse me, Lord, I know You're omniscient and all—I say this with great reverence, of course—but I'm afraid You have called the wrong person. As Your all-seeing eyes roamed the earth searching hearts and making plans, I'm afraid You missed something. Here, let me list all my limitations and weaknesses, since You must have overlooked them."

Isn't this what you and I want to say when we feel pushed by God? When we are forced to face a challenge or a change?

It wasn't just Jeremiah, Gideon, and Moses who responded in this way. We could also look at Sarah, called to be the mother of nations, who laughed—*laughed!*—in the face of God's promises: "After I am worn out and my lord is old, will I now have this pleasure?" (Genesis 18:12). Or Saul, the first king of Israel, who got so nervous on the day of his coronation that they found him hiding among the luggage. Or Zechariah the priest (and soon-to-be father of John the Baptist), who doubted the message of an angel (never a good move). Or Simon Peter, who when faced with the power of Christ, cried, "Go away from me, Lord; I am a sinful man!" (Luke 5:8).

Everyone offered excuses. Everyone felt insecure and afraid. Everyone thought God had picked the wrong person:

Jeremiah was too young.

Sarah too old.

Gideon too afraid.

Samuel too inexperienced.

Moses too shy.

Peter too rash.

And yet God used them all. We call them heroes.

Now I want to show you something in scripture, something that may make a few of your neurons explode. Let's take a look, word for word, at God's responses to Jeremiah, Gideon, and Moses.

When Jeremiah said, "Ah, Lord, I am too young" (Hebrew expert that I am, I would probably translate this more like, "Aaahhh, Lord!"), God said, "Do not say, 'I am too young.' You must go to everyone I send you to and say whatever I command you. Do not be afraid of them, for *I am with you* and will rescue you" (Jeremiah 1:7–8, emphasis added).

When Gideon finished listing his inadequacies and detailing his family's inferiority, God said, "*I will be with you*, and you will strike down all the Midianites, leaving none alive" (Judges 6:16, emphasis added).

When Moses begged, "Please send someone else," God's very first words in response were "I will be with you" (Exodus 3:12).

Do you see it? How God responded to different people with different excuses in the *exact same way*? Every time they pointed out their own weakness, sin, inferiority, or inexperience, He simply said, "I am with you."

It didn't matter who God was calling. It didn't matter where they came from or where their faith was in that moment; God's answer was the same for each of them. God's answer was *God*.

And this tells us something profound, a fear-taming, game-changing, life-giving truth: God's call wasn't about the people He called—*God's call was about Him*. It was and is and ever will be about Him.

God's call isn't about our age, our experience, our qualifications, our giftedness, our skill set, our appearance, our intelligence, our education, our heritage, our connections, our bank balance, our college transcript, our curriculum vitae, our marital status, our family background, our track record, our level of influence, our social media following. Nor is it about our character traits—courage, integrity, wisdom. Nor is it about our spiritual résumé—faith level, failures, triumphs.

God's call is about God. It is about God being with His people. And guess what? God was—as He still is and always will be—fully qualified.

God is old enough. Wise enough. Smart enough. Rich enough. Experienced enough. Educated enough. Influential enough. Successful enough. Righteous enough. Confident enough. Brave enough.

It didn't matter if Jeremiah, Moses, Gideon—or any of the people God called in the pages of scripture—were qualified, because God was with them, and that was the only qualification they needed. When God is with you, you are qualified for your call. When God is with you, you have all you need.

Do you hear this? *Really* hear this?

When God calls you, it's not about you—it's about Him. When challenge and change come our way, we can rise to meet them with confidence, courage, and a (mostly) cool head—because He is with us. When God calls us to go—to move, give, or grow in some new way—He is with us, and He is all we need.

The Problem with Self-Esteem

We talk a lot about self-esteem in today's world. Our cultural emphasis on positive self-esteem has taught us to expect—more, to need—affirmation. And honestly? The rise of social media with its encouragement to acquire large numbers of friends, followers, and likes has increased our natural desire for validation and encouragement.

When God calls me to something new, here's how my internal dialogue with Him usually goes (to be clear, I don't audibly hear God's voice—just humor my writer's imagination here):

God: "Hey, Elizabeth, I have new things for you to do. Scary things. I am calling you to write books about your weaknesses. I want you to put your worst self out there in front of thousands of strangers where you might be misunderstood, criticized, even ostracized. I want you to share about your doubts and insecurities and failures, overcome your fear of conflict and your desire to please, and call other people higher." (*Flashes a big grin and a thumbs-up.*)

Me (*returning His grin, like a four-year-old trying to charm candy out of her father*): "But Lord. . .can't I just write novels instead? Can't I hide behind my fiction? It's way safer. See, I am uncomfortable being weak. I hate looking bad. Trusting people with my vulnerabilities makes me feel. . .well, vulnerable. I'm kind of a private person. I dread being misunderstood. I fear rejection. And I hate conflict—like, can't-eat-can't-sleep hate it. All that to say. . . I'm not humble enough. Not tough enough. Not brave enough."

Me to myself: *Here's the part where God rebuts all my self-criticism. Here's the part where He plays the role of divine maternal comforter who builds me up. Or maybe the sympathetic best friend who sees the best in me and points out the good stuff I don't always see. Or maybe He'll give me a "Go-get-'em-beloved-daughter-you-will-rock-this" pep talk like the ones my parents used to give me growing up.*

I sit waiting with my humble face on. Waiting to be encouraged. Waiting to be lifted up. Waiting for God to list all the reasons He chose me. Me, only me, wonderful me, out of all seven billion people on earth. All the reasons why I—only I—am fully and uniquely qualified. Why I am righteous and gifted and perfect for the job.

God smiles and I lean forward, eager for reassurance and maybe a compliment or two. Ready for a long speech. He puts a hand on mine and says, "I will be with you."

Long pause in which I blink a lot and try to keep my expression neutral, which is stupid, seeing as God can read my expressions and my thoughts, but I do it anyway.

Me: "That's it? Your entire speech? Didn't You. . .leave out a few parts?"

God (*raising an eyebrow*): "Which parts?"

Me (*feeling more idiotic with every word*): "You know, the parts about how silly I am to be so insecure because You believe in me and think I'm—uh, great, I guess—and how You could have chosen a bajillion other people, but Your eyes searched the earth and landed on me, because—because—" *I falter, feeling heat in my cheeks, mumbling the last words.* "I'm special. . . ?" *My voice trails off till I end on an embarrassed whisper. I bury my face in my hands, more confused than ever.*

God (*tipping my chin up and smiling into my eyes*): "Don't you see? None of that matters. What matters is that *I will be with you. I will help you.*"

Me: "But do You mean—do You mean I don't matter?"

God (*chuckling a little*): "Of course you matter. But this isn't about you. It's about Me. It's about Me fulfilling My purposes through you."

I must look discouraged still because He says, "Don't you see, Elizabeth? This takes all the pressure off you. You can stop worrying so much about yourself. About making mistakes. About being imperfect. You can quit obsessing over your qualifications, your weaknesses, your sins, your regrets, your past. You, you, you."

And as He speaks, something releases inside. A pressure, a tension I didn't even know I'd been feeling. I roll His words around inside my mind: *It's not about me. It's about Him.*

He squeezes my hand and continues: "You can stop trying to do and be and figure out everything all the time. All you have to do is follow My lead. Follow and obey. Do what I have called you to do. And guess what? I know follow-and-obey is harder than it sounds, so I will give you the Holy Spirit to *help* you follow and obey!"

I open my mouth, about to reel off more objections, more self-criticism, but God holds up a palm. "Elizabeth, I know you are about to say, 'But Lord, I'm not ready for this.' I know who you are and where you are in your spiritual growth. (I'm omniscient, remember?) I called you now *even though I know you aren't ready yet.* I like it that way, because your weakness reveals My strength and brings Me glory. I decided to call you now because it's time, and because I am with you." Again He flashes the big Fatherly grin.

I am with you. These are God's words to all of us when He calls us to rise to challenge and change. When He calls us to move, to give, and to grow in new ways. To go somewhere new. To do something scary. To be something more.

Maybe God is calling you. . .

To confront a sin.

To forgive an enemy.

To raise a family.

To lead a ministry.

To deliver a message.

To adopt a child.

To share with a neighbor.

To love a difficult person.

To take on a new responsibility.

To be brave in your work.

To risk your heart in a new friendship.

To love again after heartbreak.

To be courageous enough to seek counseling.

To leave your comfortable life to do something challenging for Him.

If God has called you to do something for Him, you can have every confidence that He is with you and will provide what you lack. As Paul puts it in a letter to the Philippian church, "In all my prayers for all of you, I always pray with joy because of your partnership in the gospel from the first day until now, being confident of this, that he who began a good work in you will carry it on to completion until the day of Christ Jesus" (Philippians 1:4–6).

He will carry it—He will carry *you*—on to completion. He won't just say, "Ready, set, go!"—and then abandon you halfway through the race. He will see you through the part where legs grow tired and lungs scream for mercy. He will see you all the way to the finish line.

This means that we can say along with Paul, "We are always confident" (2 Corinthians 5:6). Can you imagine losing the chains of insecurity that have kept you bound for so long? No longer feeling hampered by your own limitations or held back by the fear of what others think? When we live our life devoted to fulfilling God's purposes, we stop worrying about ourselves: our success, our reputation, our appearance. We lose ourselves in Him. In His purpose. In His call. We seek only to hear those blessed words at life's end: "Well done, good and faithful servant!" (Matthew 25:21).

A New Way of Thinking: But God

Being called by God doesn't mean we won't face opposition, setback, and even what feels like failure along the way. Take a walk through the pages of Jeremiah and you'll see what I mean: poor Jeremiah had a rough road—a long road—to walk as God's prophet. In his decades serving as God's prophet, Jeremiah was beaten, betrayed, imprisoned, and tossed into a muddy cistern to starve. He was called a liar, fraud, and traitor. He even wore a yoke—no, not a metaphorical one. God had Jeremiah build a yoke and wear it around his neck to prove a point!

Being called by God doesn't come with the promise, "And then everything will be easy and perfect and you'll live happily ever after!" Nope. Fulfilling God's call may be challenging—maybe even the most challenging thing we've ever faced. But we can face it, we can rise to meet it, we can cross that finish line. With God's help, we can see His call to completion.

Do you see how this simplifies things for us? God's job is to run the universe and set aside good works for us. Our job is to set aside our own fears and agendas so God can do what He wills to us, in us, and through us. When God calls us to something new, instead of saying, "But Lord, I (insert fear, insecurity, limitation, excuse, or objection here)," we get to say, "But God can."

Instead of "But Lord, I am nobody," God wants us to say, "But God is Somebody."

Instead of "But Lord, I am too sinful," God wants us to say, "But God is with me."

Instead of "But Lord, I am too inexperienced," God wants us to say, "But God knows what to do."

Instead of "But Lord, I have made too many mistakes," God wants us to say, "But God turns weakness into strength" (see 2 Corinthians 12:7–10).

Instead of "But Lord, I can't," God wants us to say, "But God can."

Let's take "But Lord, I—" and turn it into "But God can."

Fear "Disorders"

When we say—when we believe—"But God can," He helps us overcome the fears that plague us. Maybe some of these fear "disorders" will sound familiar:

- Too Good to Be True Syndrome
- Hyperactive Self-Criticism Condition
- God Made a Mistake Disorder
- Just Kidding I Didn't Mean to Pray That Prayer Disease (because now God said yes and I have to be brave)
- That's Too Scary So I Won't Even Try It Disorder (which is closely related to. . .)
- That's Too Hard So Let's Pretend God Didn't Say It Disorder
- If I Don't Try I Can't Fail Syndrome
- I've Been Hurt Before So I'd Rather Stay Safe Disease

I'm not making these things up—I have been plagued by every one at some point in my life. (*Ahem.* I faced every single one *while writing this book.*) How about you? Without God's help, these issues can become permanent prisons, lifelong afflictions, but "with God all things are possible" (Matthew 19:26). Maybe on our own we can't overcome these fears, *but God can.*

Before You Were Born

When God called Jeremiah, He said, "Before I formed you in the womb I knew you, before you were born I set you apart; I appointed you as a prophet to the nations" (Jeremiah 1:5). God had a vision for Jeremiah's life before he was even born. You may be thinking, *Well, of course He did. Jeremiah was a prophet. He was special. He wrote a book of the Bible, for crying out loud. Me? I'm just. . .me.*

Well, *just you*, take a look at the following passage, which is for all Christians everywhere. In his letter to the Ephesian church, Paul writes this truth:

> *Thus he shows for all time the tremendous generosity of the grace and kindness he has expressed towards us in Christ Jesus. It was nothing you could or did achieve—it was God's gift to you. No one can pride himself upon earning the love of God. The fact is that what we are we owe to the hand of God upon us. We are born afresh in Christ, and born to do those good deeds which God planned for us to do.*
>
> EPHESIANS 2:8–10 PHILLIPS

It wasn't just Jeremiah; God saw you and me before we were born too. God started making plans for us before our mothers even knew we were coming.

Let's just sit here for a second while our neurons set off some fireworks. Because this is a mind-blowing truth, is it not? One of those thoughts that, if you think about it for too long, makes you dizzy.

God called you before you were born. God has purposes for you. Good works for you to perform. Roles and responsibilities for you to fulfill. He's been planning them for a long time. Setting them up for you. Moving things around to get them ready. And on the day you were born, I picture Him watching from heaven, cheering and rubbing His almighty hands together and saying to Jesus, "I've been waiting for this one. She's got a lot I need her to do. Now we can get started."

Some of us picture that scene and feel inspired—*Really? God needs me? God wants me? My life matters?* We read it and feel valuable, useful, excited. And that's how God wants us to feel! We are designed to do good works. We were made for a reason, and we have important work to do for our Creator!

But when others of us read this, although we experience a flash of excitement and joy, it is quickly doused by a wet blanket of pressure. *Oh great,* we think, *here we go. I always knew this grace thing was too good to be true. I knew there were strings attached. God has an agenda. He expects something out of me—something I'll never be able to give. Doesn't He know who I am? How sinful, how inexperienced?*

And, of course, now we have circled back to the beginning of Jeremiah's conversation with God—the self-focus. The "But Lord."

You've Been Prequalified

Last summer, after five years spent living in borrowed houses with our future uncertain and our hearts on edge, afraid to put down roots in case we had to move again, my husband and I were finally ready to buy a house. We'd had our eye on a particular house for months, and when we finally got a definitive answer about our future, we wasted no time. We started making calls.

And here's the thing: Houses are expensive. (Duh.) Kevin and I didn't have the thousands upon thousands of dollars we needed to buy the house. But we had access to a bank, and *that bank* has thousands upon thousands of dollars. So before we ever made an offer on the house, we spoke to the bank, they looked at our salaries, and based on our salaries and credit history (and, I like to pretend, our good looks and charm), they prequalified us for a loan. By ourselves, we didn't have what it took to buy the house, but the bank had what was needed; and because of the bank's qualifications, Kevin and I were also qualified. Qualified ahead of time, in fact—before we ever made an offer on the house. We were prequalified.

When God calls you to fulfill a "good work" He has in mind for your life, you may not have all the qualities and qualifications you need, but God does. And when God calls you, you can be sure of this: You have been prequalified. He Himself will put up whatever you need to help you fulfill your part. God Himself is investing in your future. What you lack, He will loan. What you need, He will provide.

The Bible puts it this way: "For those God foreknew he also predestined to be conformed to the image of his Son, that he might be the firstborn among many brothers and sisters. And those he predestined, he also called; those he called, he also justified; those he justified, he also glorified" (Romans 8:29–30). When God has plans for your life, He calls you; and when God calls you, He provides what you need: justification and, one day, glorification.

Peter elaborates: "His divine power has given us everything we need for a godly life through our knowledge of him who called us by his own glory and goodness" (2 Peter 1:3). By His own glory and goodness (not ours!) God called us, and then He provided *everything we would need* to fulfill that call—to live a godly life.

Of course, being prequalified doesn't mean "free ride with no responsibilities." Kevin and I still have to pay our monthly bills. Hold jobs so we can hold up our part of the deal. The analogy falters a bit here: We don't do good works for God to earn salvation or God's affection (as we saw in Ephesians 2:8)—no, we don't need to earn those, nor do we need to repay them. God gives His salvation and affection freely and lavishly, and they were paid for—fully paid for—by the blood of Christ. But even so, once we are saved, we all have work to do. Our Maker created us to crave purpose and meaning, and He has assigned us each a set of tasks and roles that will give us that fulfillment—and serve His purposes along the way.

When God prequalifies us for a purpose, part of fulfilling that purpose means we put our hands to the proverbial plow: we expand our skills, we push ourselves, we take steps of faith. . .all the while knowing that God is behind us, giving us all we need to meet the challenge.

So let's bring this into the real world.

Let's say that before you were born, God set aside a person with whom He wanted you to share the Gospel. Even if you have never helped someone come to faith before, God has prequalified you for the job. What wisdom you lack, He will provide. He will provide in different ways: through scripture, the Holy Spirit, and the guidance of partners and mentors in Christ who can help you, equip you, and hold up your arms.

Let's say that before you were born, God envisioned you in a certain career that would bring Him glory. . .you were prequalified.

That student He wants you to tutor. . .prequalified.

That ministry He wants you to lead. . .prequalified.

That book He wants you to write. . .prequalified.

That hurting soul He wants you to befriend. . .prequalified.

That difficult child He wants you to raise. . .prequalified.

Because of Him.

Because God is qualified.

Because God.

Because God. Those two words change everything about how we respond to God's call. When the evil voice of doubt whispers, "Why this? Why now? Why me?" we need only say, "Because God."

God called Jeremiah in his youth, and even though Jeremiah was afraid, he answered the call. He felt unprepared and ill-equipped—too young, not ready—but that didn't matter to God. God was with Jeremiah, and *that* was all that mattered. Jeremiah's role as prophet was not easy. Not glamorous. He didn't get a mega-church, a TV show, or a book deal. His obedience brought him critics and conflict, prison and persecution. It nearly got him killed several times. Jeremiah wrote, "The word of the LORD has brought me insult and reproach all day long. But if I say, 'I will not mention his word or speak anymore in his name,' his word is in my heart like a fire, a fire shut up in my bones. I am weary of holding it in; indeed, I cannot" (Jeremiah 20:8–9).

If you have felt called—pushed, encouraged, stretched—by God, but have hung back, hiding behind a list of excuses and insecurities, I pray you hang back no more. I pray you take your eyes off yourself and put them on God. God who is always qualified—more than qualified. God whose qualifications you can borrow. God who has already prequalified you for any role He wants you to fill.

God planned, God called, and Jeremiah answered. He had many weak moments of doubt and insecurity and loneliness along the way, but he did not give up. In Jeremiah 17:16 he declares, "I have not run away from being your shepherd." Jeremiah fulfilled the purpose for which he was born, the deeds to which he had been called. Jeremiah answered God's call. He turned his "But Lord, I—" into "But God can." He did it, and *because God* is with us, so can we.

Let's Go Deeper. . .

For Further Study
Jeremiah 17 reveals the source of Jeremiah's strong faith even through great difficulty.

Journal Prompt
1. Fill in the blank: "Ah, Lord, I am too _____." Can you find a scripture to help you view that "limitation" from God's perspective?
2. Which "fear disorder(s)" do you struggle with?

3. What specific purposes do you think God has in mind for your life?

Prayer Prompt
*I prayed to the L*ORD*, and he answered me.*
       He freed me from all my fears.
Those who look to him for help will be radiant with joy;
       no shadow of shame will darken their faces.
*In my desperation I prayed, and the L*ORD *listened;*
       he saved me from all my troubles.
PSALM 34:4–6 NLT

3
When Your Past Is against You

Mary Magdalene's Story

Based on John 20:11–18

It haunts her once more. The waiting shadow, the hungry darkness. Always just out of sight, just outside of human hearing, a darting enemy that hides every time she turns her head. But here just before dawn, with morning mist—night's last gasp—uncoiling from the earth, snaking around her ankles, she senses it wants to pull her under. *They* want to pull her under. She hasn't felt the presence, heard the voice, seen the shadow for many months, but now, with her Protector gone, she fears they will come for her. Come to reclaim their lost property.

I knew it was all too good to be true. People like me don't get to find home. People like me don't get to go free.

She shudders.

Stop it, Mary, she tells herself—but even the voice in her mind sounds shaky, unconvincing. *Jesus told them never to come back. Jesus said you were free.*

She clings to the memory for strength:

That first day when He found her huddling in the filthy shadows of a rotting side street. The day everything changed. His voice, driving them out. Her shock, making her bold, so bold she looked up and met a man's gaze. His gaze. The softness in His eyes—was that a smile?—as He held out a hand and pulled her to her feet. The way He looked *at* her, not through her. The way He saw *her*, not just. . .them. The mess they had left behind. How, even then with the fog in her mind still clearing, she knew He saw her for the woman she could be, not the woman she was. And in Him she saw kindness, hope, and—somehow—home.

"What is your name?" He asked that day.

"M–Mary," she whispered, through a throat dry from disuse.

"Mary," He said, and her name had never sounded so beautiful—on His lips, it was almost a song. "Mary," He repeated, one side of His mouth quirking in a smile. "One of my favorite names."

Now, from a dark corner of her mind comes a quiet voice, more hiss than words: *Jesus also said you could depend on Him. And now He is gone.*

"Stop it," she says aloud, through gritted teeth. "He said I was free—forever free—and He would not lie." She runs to catch up with the other women, her friends. *Will they still be your friends now that Jesus is gone?* She feels a stab of guilt for such selfish thoughts—her thoughts should be all about Jesus, all about His suffering, His death—but even grief cannot be simple for her. Even her grief is tainted.

The women pick their way across damp fields toward the cliff that houses Jesus' tomb. The spices in Mary's pack are heavy, cloying; perhaps they would smell pleasant if they did not remind her so forcibly of death. Loss. Despair.

But as sunrise unspools along the hills, a golden thread, the women stop, shocked into silence. The tomb gapes open, a dark mouth yawning from the side of the hill. The huge stone, rolled aside. The Roman guard, gone. And two shining men, their clothes gleaming white-hot, standing beside it.

The women hurry to tell the others. Peter comes running, John comes running, no one understands. As the others leave, Mary lingers. She looks inside: empty tomb, folded clothes. She walks out to the garden, paces circles in the dirt. Shoves a fist in her mouth, tries to quiet her cries.

Every sound makes her jump—have they come for her so soon? She doesn't want the other women to see her like this—undone, grasping at hope. She should be stronger after so long with Him, so long drinking in His faith and His words. She should be strong like they are, but for her it's so much darker than grief. . . .

A stick snaps behind her. With a gasp she whirls, expecting shadow. Instead she sees a man. The sun is rising behind him, angling up in golden-fingered rays. It lights his outline, blurs his features, hurts her eyes. She blinks, half-blinded.

"Woman, why are you crying? Who is it you are looking for?"

Relief spills warm inside. This is a man's voice, not a demon's. She squints at him, trying to see past the light. His clothes are covered in a rust-colored crust. Perhaps he is the gardener. She averts her eyes from his face, as propriety requires. "Sir, if you have carried Him away, tell me where you have put Him, and I will get Him."

The man steps forward, out of the sun's glare. "Mary."

She would know that song anywhere.

"Teacher?" Wonder, shock, joy, and a thousand questions surge, setting her trembling. She looks straight into His face. There the familiar smile, there the soft brown eyes. The same eyes she had seen glassy and empty when they took His body down from the cross just three days earlier.

"Teacher!" Her voice a girlish squeal. She stumbles forward, falling to her knees, reaching for His feet. His bloodstained, mangled, precious feet. She wets them with her tears.

A hand rests gentle on her shoulder, and she looks up. "Do not hold on to Me," He says, but she only clings tighter, cries harder, "for I have not yet returned to the Father. Go instead to My brothers and tell them, 'I am returning to My Father and your Father, to My God and your God.'"

"M—me?" she stammers. "You want *me* to deliver this message?"

He nods. "Yes, Mary." His smile warms her, lights her, all the way through, driving away all the shadows—even the fear of shadows. "I need you. I need you to do this for Me." When she hesitates, His eyes crinkle. "Mary, I will see you again. But now I need you to do this for Me. I need you to go."

Heart soaring, Mary flies.

One line, not even a full sentence—that's the only description we get of Mary Magdalene's life before Jesus: "Mary (called Magdalene) from whom seven demons had come out" (Luke 8:2). What a history that short line suggests. A woman haunted by seven demons probably didn't have friends. She had probably abandoned—or more likely, been abandoned by—her family. Perhaps she had nowhere left to go.

Although we know little about Mary's life before Jesus, we know that after Jesus, her life was *all* Jesus. He Himself became her home. The Gospels mention her often among the women who traveled with Jesus and the Twelve, caring for their needs. And so when Jesus died that awful day—when darkness fell in broad daylight, the Light of the World extinguished on a wooden cross—Mary would have been left not just brokenhearted, but also terrified.

Now what? Now where could she go? Would her newfound friends disperse and hide, leaving her to fend for herself? And if Mary's heart was left empty, would her demons return?

But then comes Sunday. Sunday, glorious Sunday! A heart once more beating, a stone rolled away. Although Jesus has conquered death and vanquished Satan, He does not return as Roman victors did. Instead of trumpets in streets we find tears in a garden; instead of crowds of admirers we find one lonely woman.

It is astounding that Jesus appears first to Mary Magdalene. Some might say it was a bad idea. If you are Jesus and you are looking to orchestrate an incontrovertible resurrection timeline, to give the skeptics an impressive lineup of eyewitnesses. . .well, Mary Magdalene as first witness is not the way to go. First, she is a woman, and in Jesus' day her testimony would not hold the same weight as a man's. Second, she is a woman with a questionable background, an untrustworthy witness. *The first witness to the so-called resurrection is a person who was once possessed by seven demons? Oh, and that person is a woman? Riiiight.*

Jesus could have done this so many other ways. So why appear first to Mary Magdalene? Perhaps it was this simple—and this beautiful: Because she needed it most. She needed *Him* most. The first witness to the resurrection was a woman who had been brought back from a living death, a woman who needed to know that Jesus' promises hadn't been empty. Her "resurrection" hadn't been too good to be true after all. It was all true, *still* true; Jesus would go on living—and now so could she.

And ponder this: Why appear to Mary alone? Why wait for everyone else to leave? Why set up Mary's story to be doubted, with no one else present to corroborate her story?

Again, I suspect this was deliberate on Jesus' part. This was a gift, His parting gift to His mourning, still vulnerable friend. Here in the garden, in the silence of a gold-tipped sunrise, Mary got one last moment alone with her Lord.

And in this small space, the woman who likely bore more emotional and spiritual wounds than any of Jesus' other followers was first to embrace the risen Lord with His wounds. *If He can rise to live again with His scars, then surely so can I.* In this heartrending reunion we find hope for all of us who live with scars, all who come limping into the kingdom of God, seeking healing and hope.

Such extraordinary kindness! Such intimate grace! Such poignant testimony to the kind of God we serve. The kind of friend we find in Jesus. The kind of friend who takes us with our wounds, our scars, our fears, and loves us each the way we need to be loved.

When Mugs Break

I toss my keys onto the counter and sink into my friend Emma's cushy new love seat with a grateful sigh: "How can eight hours of sitting in a car leave you so exhausted? Let the girlfriends' weekend begin. . . I just have to wake up first."

"This should do the trick." With a smile, Emma's husband Kim presses a steaming mug of British tea into my hands.

"You are the *best*," I tell him.

I cradle the mug, savoring the way warmth travels from the pottery, through my fingertips, into my soul. Emma asks what I want to do tomorrow. I lift the mug to my lips, gathering thoughts.

In the silence between sentences there's a strange crunching sound, and suddenly I'm burning. Scalding tea is everywhere—drenching my hands, filling my lap, soaking the chair. I yelp and leap to my feet. In one bleeding hand I hold the mug's handle; in the other I'm struggling to balance the now half-empty mug. The next moments are a blur of shrieks and towels, bandages and blood. When the pain stops and the chaos settles, we register what happened: the handle separated from the mug, sending tea flying and pottery shards digging into my hand.

Eventually, when we realize that there's more blood than actual injury, that my clothes have protected me from burns, and that Emma's forethought in stain-protecting her new love seat has kept the furniture from total ruin, we dissolve into shaky, relieved laughter.

I change clothes, we clean up, and after a while we are back where we started, settling in to chat on the couches. Kim brews a fresh cup of tea and holds it out to me. For a heartbeat I hesitate—a hitch of anxiety stops my breath—then slowly I reach out to take the mug. As we talk I find myself holding the mug harder than I should be, pressing it tight between both hands. I cast nervous glances at the handle, studying its width, weighing its strength. In spite of the rational voice in my head insisting, "This is so stupid—hold the handle," I can't bring myself to do it.

The next morning, Emma offers me coffee. Coffee, beloved coffee, sweet nectar of life. She pours me a cup and holds out the mug. A fluttering starts in my gut, and I find myself swallowing hard as I reach out with my still-bandaged hand. She reads the fear on my face. "Are you okay?"

I nod my head yes. Shake my head no. Confess with a laugh, "I'm afraid to pick up the mug!"

Emma laughs, then pretends to be wounded. "You don't trust my mugs anymore."

"Not *your* mugs," I say with a guilty grin. "Mugs in general."

Emma assures me that the mug in question has been a reliable vessel for coffee and tea for years and is worthy of my full trust. She holds it herself, waves it around to demonstrate. We laugh, I pretend to feel better, and I pick up the cup, hoping she doesn't notice that I'm using two hands, unwilling to risk the handle.

Several days later I return home—home to my own coffeepot and my own familiar mugs, dear companions who have faithfully served me coffee and tea during countless prayer times, phone calls, and writing sessions. But even so, when I pour my first cup of coffee into my favorite mug, the "Our nest is blessed" bird mug my mom gave me, I find myself staring it down with narrowed eyes, suspicion rising: *Are you going to fail me too? Are you hiding some unseen crack, some weakness in construction? We've lived a lot of life together, shared a lot of coffee and good memories, but now. . .I've been burned. I've changed—have you changed too?*

Over the next few weeks, I keep drinking coffee, but always with two hands, just in case. The two-handed mug-hold becomes an unconscious habit. Even though logic tells me I'm being ridiculous—*In all your thirty-eight years you have had three million positive experiences drinking from mugs, and only one bad experience with mug malfunction—the odds are in your favor!*—every time I lift a mug, some primal instinct rises up to defend me. To keep me from getting burned. Keep me using two hands.

After a while it occurs to me that I've done this before, only not with mugs. With people. With God. Most of my life has been filled with love, kindness, grace—ten million wondrous memories—but along the way I've also experienced a few shocking hurts and disappointments. Wounds I didn't see coming, from places I'd never doubted.

Sometimes things break on us—not just mugs, but things that

really matter: Health. Sanity. Friendships. Finances. Churches. Parents. Marriages. Families.

Things we thought were a given, things we trusted without question—*my mug will always hold my coffee, my friend will always be there, my church will always be a safe place, my parents will always love each other, my guy will always be faithful, my body will always be healthy*—suddenly let us down. They break without warning. One minute we're sitting on a couch with a friend—happy place, familiar comfort—the next we're gasping in pain, world spinning, and it's ages before we can even register what happened.

When we're surprised like that, when things break on us, sometimes *we* break too. And soon trust is overcome by fear. Love is overshadowed by suspicion. Openness is overwhelmed by hurt.

Like Mary, we don't want to be broken. We're not doing it on purpose. Logically, we tell ourselves that our newfound fear makes no sense—in neutral moments we might even laugh at ourselves—but every time we face situations that somehow remind us of *that one terrible time*, the fear comes boiling to the surface. Taking over. Commandeering our thoughts, our feelings, our reactions. Making us curl into a self-protective cocoon where we can hide safe inside, safe all alone.

We who used to live free, love hard. . .we become guarded. Protective. Isolated. Maybe angry.

We are not crazy, not making it up. Some broken things, like my friend's mug, are beyond hope and have to be thrown away, and those losses hurt beyond words. Other broken things can be repaired, but repair is scary. Imperfect. Risky. Even if we manage to glue the handle back, we still see a seam. A scar. A weak place that we fear could break again.

If things or people have broken on you, if you yourself are broken, these words are for you. You know pain, suspicion, fear—so did Mary Magdalene. So do I. At times we have all been chained by our past, shackled by fear, so that even when we have *wanted* to answer God's call, we couldn't.

With God, Weakness Has Purpose

Here's a truth we have to embrace if we ever want to heal—from fear, from hurt, from sin, from any kind of brokenness: God chose us *because of our weakness*. Drink in this encouraging passage from Paul's first letter to the church in Corinth—a broken church if ever there was one:

> *Remember, dear brothers and sisters, that few of you*
> *were wise in the world's eyes or powerful or wealthy*
> *when God called you. Instead, God chose things*
> *the world considers foolish in order to shame those*
> *who think they are wise. And he chose things that*
> *are powerless to shame those who are powerful. God*
> *chose things despised by the world, things counted*
> *as nothing at all, and used them to bring to nothing*
> *what the world considers important. As a result, no*
> *one can ever boast in the presence of God.*
>
> 1 CORINTHIANS 1:26–29 NLT

Foolish. Powerless. Despised. Counted as nothing. If you have ever felt like those words describe you, then first, welcome to the We're All Unworthy Club, and second, rejoice in knowing that your weakness brings all the more glory to God!

The Shackles of Shame

Some of us have become Christians—free people, coheirs with our older brother Jesus—and yet we still live as prisoners. The gift of baptism has allowed us to participate in the death, burial, and resurrection of Jesus (Romans 6:1–4), and for about five minutes afterward, we danced around feeling free. But then came doubt. Fear. The insidious voice of the enemy, whispering, *You are forgiven, but barely. The stain on your soul remains.* And we promptly sat back down and handcuffed ourselves to a chair, because we can't be trusted.

Regret and shame are shackles we put on ourselves even after Christ has removed them. They paralyze us:

- I may be saved, but I am not worthy to speak for Christ.
- I am not worthy to do anything great for God. The best I can hope for is just to make it through.
- God can't really use someone like me, with all my baggage—in fact, I am an energy drain. God is going to expend a lot of church resources just getting me to heaven. I'm doomed to always be a taker. I have nothing valuable to give.
- I may be going to heaven, but barely. Just making it through the pearly gates is the best I can hope for. I'm one of those "by the hair of my chinny-chin-chin" Christians.
- I can't ask for more than simple salvation. I used up my entire allotment of grace just getting my ticket to heaven—there's no way I am getting anything beyond the most basic of blessings.
- I've made terrible mistakes even as a Christian. I know I've repented and I'm forgiven and all, but I think God wants me to spend a few years pondering those mistakes, feeling bad about them, reliving them, and reminding Him how horrible I feel about them—then maybe I will earn my forgiveness.

It's easier to see through these lies when we see them printed like this in black and white, but they sound convincing when Satan whispers them in our minds and hearts, don't they? (And by the way, there's a lesson in that: If you struggle with believing lies about your forgiveness and worthiness, write them down and speak them aloud to God and to a godly friend. Lies lose power when they escape our heads and are exposed to the light of day—more, to the light of Christ. See John 3:19–21.)

The Bible calls Satan our accuser. He takes great joy in recounting our sins before God. Reminding Him of our many failures. But Jesus has overthrown Satan, robbed him of power:

> *Then I heard a loud voice in heaven say: "Now have come the salvation and the power and the kingdom of our God, and the authority of his Messiah. For the accuser of our brothers and sisters, who accuses them before our God day and night, has been hurled down."*
>
> REVELATION 12:10

Jesus' death threw Satan down (the ultimate throw-down!), but even so, even after Jesus has saved us, we can still hear the accuser's voice. Still believe his twisted truth.

When we become Christians, He not only takes away our guilt; He also takes away our *shame*. We don't just get out of jail; God wipes clean our criminal record. We don't even get assigned a parole officer to check in on us. Take a look at these soaring scriptures:

> *Jesus replied, "Very truly I tell you, everyone who sins is a slave to sin. Now a slave has no permanent place in the family, but a son belongs to it forever. So if the Son sets you free, you will be free indeed."*
>
> JOHN 8:34–36

Free indeed, my friend. *Free indeed.* That's us when we are covered in the blood of the Lamb. But wait! There's more:

> *For he chose us in him before the creation of the world to be holy and blameless in his sight. In love he predestined us for adoption to sonship through*

Jesus Christ, in accordance with his pleasure and will—to the praise of his glorious grace, which he has freely given us in the One he loves. In him we have redemption through his blood, the forgiveness of sins, in accordance with the riches of God's grace that he lavished on us.

EPHESIANS 1:4–8

Did you catch that word there in verse 4—*blameless*? Blameless means no guilt. No shame. No regret. Now tell me, is that how you feel? Because it's how Christians should feel! And get this—*it's how our loving Father wants us to feel*. He spent millennia and gave His Son's life in purchasing this expensive gift, this "lavish" gift, for us; let us not now despise the gift by refusing it. By devaluing it. By saying, "Thanks, but no thanks. I can't accept this. Don't you know I'm not worthy?" Of course we're not worthy! *No one is.* Our unworthiness is the whole point. Let us not allow God's generous grace to go to waste. Yes, it is precious and priceless, and no, we don't deserve it—but let us accept and enjoy it. Grace is a gift and it is fully ours.

Imagine this scenario: One snowy Christmas morning, a little girl receives a present under the tree: elaborately wrapped, her name written in fancy script—her father's hand—on the card. She opens it and gasps in amazement. It is beautiful, perfect, priceless. For a few minutes, she takes it out, hugs it to her chest, and smiles as her happy parents watch. But after a few minutes, the light fades from her eyes. The smile falls from her face. With a deep sigh, she carefully wraps the gift back up in its paper, seals the box, and tucks the gift into a dark corner of her closet. Out of reach, out of sight. A few days later, her father comes to her and asks, "Where is your gift? Are you not enjoying it?"

With tears in her eyes, the child says, "It's everything I ever hoped for and more. But. . .I don't deserve it. I was far from perfect this year. Sometimes I was selfish. I threw a couple of pity parties when I didn't get my way. Sometimes I was rude and disrespectful.

I even told a couple of lies." Her head falls, and she refuses to meet her father's eyes. "So I've decided I don't deserve it. It needs to stay in my closet. Maybe I'll take it out one day when I deserve it."

The father ducks his head down, into her line of sight. His grin is sideways. "But darling, do you think I don't know those things about you?"

The little girl shrugs one shoulder. "I—I don't know."

The father gathers her into his arms. "I didn't buy you that gift as a reward for good behavior. I bought it because I love you and I want you to be happy."

Tears are dripping down the girl's face now. "I don't deserve to be happy."

Her father wipes them away with a thumb. "Says who?"

She buries her face into his chest where she can hear his heartbeat, strong and steady. "Says me, I guess."

Her father chuckles, and she feels the rumble of his laughter against the side of her head. "Isn't that *my* job? Deciding what you deserve?"

She sniffles into his chest. After a long pause, she says, "But it's so *expensive*."

He rests his chin on her head and speaks softly. "I know exactly how much it cost. But this is what fathers do for beloved daughters. We buy them gifts they don't deserve and can't afford."

When she doesn't respond, he says, "I put a lot of thought and all my love into buying that gift for you. I hope you'll dig it out of the closet, open the box, and enjoy it."

She tips red-rimmed eyes up to look at him. "Really?"

He smiles. "Really. Nothing would make me happier than to see my little girl enjoying the gift I bought her. And not just enjoying it a little bit—I want to see you grinning and singing and twirling around the house, smiling so big your face hurts. Do you think you can do that for me?"

She thinks hard. "I think so. . .if that's what will really make you happy."

He squeezes her tight. "Nothing would make me happier."

Sometimes we act as though God is not omniscient. As though we have been sly enough to outsmart Him, sneaky enough to weasel our way into His kingdom. We worry that if He ever found out how terrible we are—how sinful our past, how dark our darkness—He would immediately send the Angel Police to arrest us and kick us out for trespassing in His kingdom! My friend, God saved us even knowing how sinful we are—and the truth is, He grasps the heartache, the ugliness, and the pain caused by our sins even more than we do. And *even so*, He wants to save us. *Even so*, He offers His Son's pure blood on our behalf. This is amazing grace indeed.

Don't let shame keep you from going where God wants you to go. From becoming the person He has already empowered you to become.

Don't let regret keep you from moving forward. Don't let lingering feelings of guilt—feelings that are just feelings, and not reality—keep you stuck in the past. Maybe God's call to you is, "Go! Leave your past in the past and move forward with your life. Take the gift of grace I have offered you and run with it!"

Don't let shame silence you. You have a testimony—perhaps it's a messy one, filled with embarrassing stories and an R-rated past, not suitable for young audiences. . .but what glory your trans-formation can bring to the name of Christ! What praise He can receive through you and your mess!

When It's Time to Go

Mary's difficult past may have stood against her—it even may have "earned" her a private resurrection encounter, but Mary still got the call to go. "Go and tell the others," Jesus said.

Go and tell. Isn't that what it always comes back to in the end? *Come and heal. Go and tell.*

The more difficult your past, the greater your miracle. The more you have been forgiven, the more grace you have to give. The

Lord did not save you just for you. He saved you for others. So that you might go. Go with your scars, go as you heal, go and tell. Go be the light He left burning here on earth.

If you have lived a life in Christ knowing you are forgiven but not feeling fully so. . .let Mary's story set you free. Free to *be* free.

Think outside the Box

Shame and fear want us to live trapped in an invisible box of our own creation. The wounds may have come from others, but the box we built and locked ourselves—and *we still hold the key*. As you read this book, I pray you decide to use that key. Climb out of that box. Stand free in God's sun.

I am proud to say I have learned to trust mugs again. (Now *there's* a sentence that has never been written before!) Today I am grateful for the lessons the broken mug taught me: Most of the time, life is wonderful. But sometimes it hurts. People disappoint. Things change. Mugs break. But you and I. . .we can move forward. Like Mary, with God's help, we can heal. Forgive ourselves. Forgive others. In time, maybe even forget.

And you know what? Even if we can't forget, even if we still bear the scar, it's worth it, reaching out and taking hold of that mug once more. Scar or no scar, bad memories and all, the tea, the coffee, this life, they taste as good as ever.

We don't know what God did in Mary Magdalene's life after this moment in the garden with Jesus. She delivered Jesus' message to the Twelve—after that, God only knows. I picture Mary receiving the Spirit on the Day of Pentecost. I picture her among the joyful early disciples in Jerusalem, devoted to the apostles' teachings, to the breaking of bread, and to prayer (see Acts 2:42). I imagine her pooling funds to share a home with the other women who had once traveled with Jesus—Joanna, Salome, and others— filling their days with service and their nights with laughter.

And on nights when old wounds ached and sleep wouldn't come, I picture Mary lying still in her bed, eyes closed, going back in time to relive the sunrise she shared with the Lord. To see again the smile that lit His bruised face, a smile all for her. To hear again the beloved voice singing her song, saying her name. And then I picture her disobeying the last command He gave her—"Don't hang on to Me"—by hanging on to Him with all her heart. *I'm sorry, Lord, but I'm never letting go.*

Let's Go Deeper. . .

For Further Study

Read 2 Corinthians 12:1–10 and ponder how this passage connects to Mary Magdalene's life—and yours. How does God receive more glory when He works through our weakness?

Journal Prompt

1. What big things have broken on you in life, and how have you responded?
2. Have you already seen God use your weakness, sins, and brokenness for His good purposes? How might God want to use those things in the future?
3. How did you feel when you read the story of the little girl tucking her father's gift away? What gifts does your Father want you to pull out of the closet and enjoy?

Prayer Prompt

Therefore, since we have a great high priest who has ascended into heaven, Jesus the Son of God, let us hold firmly to the faith we profess. For we do not have a high priest who is unable to empathize with our weaknesses, but we have one who has been tempted in every way, just as we are—yet he did not sin. Let us then approach God's throne of grace with confidence, so that we may receive mercy and find grace to help us in our time of need.
Hebrews 4:14–16

4
When It's Time to Go All In

Peter's Story, Part 1

Based on Matthew 14:22–33

$\mathscr{P}$eter gave up on sleeping hours ago. A single lantern grants a feeble circle of orange light. It bounces, revealing splintered half images: arms straining at ropes, dark bags sliding across wet deck. Beyond the light's small warmth the cold sea writhes—a hungry mouth, oily and black. After so many hours fighting wind, shouting over waves, Peter and his friends are exhausted, wordless, moving by memory.

He's been through high winds and violent storms many times, far worse than this, so he's not scared, but he is uneasy. Partly because of the waves, but mostly because of Jesus.

"Go ahead," Jesus had insisted a few hours earlier as the Twelve loaded bags onto the boat. "I'm not coming with you." Confused, Peter had raised his eyebrows at John—*Any idea what He's doing this time?*—but John had just raised *his* eyebrows and shrugged—*Don't ask me.* They did that a lot around Jesus, Peter thought now with a wry half grin. Stand around throwing each other confused glances.

"But Lord," Peter had said, crossing his arms and speaking with forced patience, as if to a stubborn child, "how will You get across without a boat—or money? And if You *do* find a way across by morning—*which you won't*—how will we find You on the other side?"

Jesus had looked up from adjusting His red sash, the sash Peter's mother-in-law had made Him months ago, and flashed one of His I-know-something-you-don't-know smiles. "I'll get across."

Peter grunted in frustration. Sometimes the Lord was just so. . .vague.

Jesus started walking away. Peter raised his palms in mock surrender. "Have it Your way. You're in charge."

Jesus threw a grin back over one shoulder. "I'll see you in the morning."

And now it is almost morning. Night's stark black is giving way to dawn's soft gray. Peter clings to the rope he's supposed to be holding, swaying half asleep on his feet.

A shout shocks him awake. More voices join in, all shouting. Peter's heart jolts, anticipating horrors—a leak in the boat, a man overboard. He follows the voices and races to join the rest at the bow, all pointing out into the water.

Peter squints, following their fingers—and gasps. Something white is moving across the water. On top of the water. He leaps back from the edge with a startled yelp—darts his head around to make sure the other guys didn't notice—then inches forward to look again. It's too small to be a boat. Too tall to be a fish.

The men are all shouting—"Ghost!" "Demon!" "Save us!"

Somewhere in the back of his mind, Peter makes a note: *If we survive this, I have to make fun of Thomas. He screams like a child.*

"What is that thing?" Andrew says at Peter's elbow.

"I don't think it's a some*thing*," John says from Peter's other side. "It's a some*one*!"

"What?" Peter grabs the lantern and holds it aloft, casting a glowing orange ribbon across the slate-colored water. The light picks out details—human details: pale robe, open hands, and—Peter gasps—a red sash. *The* red sash. The one his mother-in-law made.

And something sparks inside. The world falls silent—gone are the shouts of the men, the roar of the waves. Time itself seems to still. In this small space it all makes sense—*He* makes sense:

Jesus, hours earlier, feeding thousands from two loaves. The weight of the basket in Peter's hands as he collected leftovers, shaking his head, chuckling, wondering at *all the bread, all over the ground*.

The sick, healed at Jesus' touch. A thousand happy tears.

The catch of fish on Peter's own boat when first he met Jesus—the catch that broke the nets and nearly sank the boat.

The night Jesus woke from a nap to shout down a storm.

Jesus' mysterious smile last night. *All* of Jesus' mysterious smiles.

And now, this—this! *Water-walking*.

Peter shouts a laugh out over the water.

He had thought he believed before, but now. . .now he knows. Jesus is Lord. Lord of bread, Lord of bodies, Lord of water—Lord of it all. Jesus is walking on water—and He is Peter's friend.

Time and sound return. Already the sky has grown a little less black, a bit more gray. Transfixed, Peter watches the Lord stroll among the waves. A smile plays at Peter's lips; a yearning pulls at his heart.

Beside Peter, Thomas is muttering, "Are we *sure* it's really Him? I need a closer look."

"Of course it's Him," says John. "See the way He walks? It's Him."

Jesus is moving farther away, about to pass them by.

To pass Peter by. To leave him wallowing ankle-deep in cold water in an old boat—when he could be out there. Out there with Him.

Again tugs the familiar thrill, the wild abandon, calling him out and pulling him under. *I want to be out there. I need to be out there.* And Peter finds himself shouting words he didn't know he was going to say, calling as loud as he can into the wind, over the waves: "Lord, if it's really You, tell me to come to You on the water!"

Everything holds its breath—the wind, the waves, the Twelve. Now the confused looks are all for *Peter*.

Jesus stops. Turns. And oh, the smile that lights His face—the proud smile, the "At last I find faith on the earth" smile—for once it is directed Peter's way.

With a huge grin and a welcoming wave, Jesus cries, "Come!"

Adrenaline surges, fire in his veins. With a whoop Peter leaps up onto the prow of the boat, one hand still clinging to a rope. His last tie to safety. He leans out—far out, as far as the rope reaches—takes a huge breath, and before he has time to think, be rational, lose courage, Peter lets out another yell and launches himself overboard. Behind him, panicked voices are shouting, "Peter!" Thomas is squealing, "Nooooo!"

His feet plunge into icy water, his ankles go in and just. . .stop. They hit something solid. On water, they *land*.

He waves his arms around, bounces up and down on his toes, testing the feel, the give, the structure of. . .whatever it is holding him up. *Water? Water!* "I'm standing on water," Peter whispers to himself.

His smile turns to a chuckle; his chuckle builds—a laugh, a rush, a roar, exploding out of him in a "Ha-*haaa!*" He throws his head back, arms wide. Rough waves slosh around his legs and slap against his waist, but he hardly feels the cold and wet. A little farther out, the Lord stands beaming at him. Jesus jerks His chin toward the writhing water beyond: *Let's go out there together.*

Eyes on Jesus, drinking in his Master's proud smile, Peter lifts one leg—again time slows; he is floating above himself, watching some other Peter do the impossible, the insane—and steps forward. Places his foot back down in the water. *On* the water. He grins at Jesus and points at his own feet: *Do You see this? Do You see me?* Jesus throws His head back and laughs.

Hooting and whooping, giddy and free, Peter takes another step. Three steps, four steps, five, he's getting closer, closing the gap, almost to Jesus.

A huge wave swells to his left. Stinging spray catches him hard in the face, momentarily blinding him. He gasps, sucking in a few icy drops. Coughing, he looks around. Wind is clawing at his head, blowing wet hair into his eyes. He looks back—he can't find the boat, only row on row of ravening waves. Another dark swell rises, tall as a house, bearing down. He turns to Jesus—wait, which way is forward, which way is back? He can't find the boat, can't find the Lord. Up comes another wave—another, still another, a relentless siege. His wife's shrill voice echoes in his mind: "Simon, what are you *doing*? Don't you ever *think*?"

And suddenly he feels it: the frigid water lapping at his ankles; the rocking, sickening motion rolling around him, beside him, beneath him. He looks down. Dark waves rise and reach. A swell slams into his torso, knocking him sideways—and he is sinking, going under, alone.

Ice water swallows his chest, bites at his neck. He is choking, freezing, floundering. "Help! Lord!" A wave smacks his face. He sucks in a mouthful of water—*Can't breathe, can't speak, going down. . .* Another wave rises—

Through the wave comes a hand, open and reaching.

Peter reaches up, desperate and drowning.

The hand is warm.

❧

"Come."

One word.

One *terrifying* word.

I bet Peter didn't think Jesus would actually say it. We know Peter (we *love* Peter), his mouth often two steps ahead of his brain. I have sometimes wondered if Peter was just talking a big game from the boat, not serious about water-walking. But then Jesus said, "Come," and things got *seriously* serious. It was time: Time to go overboard. Time to go all in.

❧

I once stood in line at a high dive at Wakulla Springs, Florida, behind a girl named Erin. It's been almost thirty years, and I still remember her name. If you've never been to a freshwater spring, you need to know three things: (1) The water is freezing. (2) The springs are deep. (3) The water is so clear, so pure, that you can see straight to the bottom. So if you stand on a twenty-foot-high diving platform looking down into water that's thirty feet deep (as we were—at least in my memory), *it looks and feels like you're about to jump fifty feet to your death.* Kind of like bungee jumping, but without the bungee.

So poor Erin got to the edge of the platform, looked down, and froze. Too scared to go forward, too proud to go back. She would creep forward a centimeter, bend a knee as if rehearsing her jumping motion. . .the kids behind her in line would hold our breath. . .then she would shake her head and back up again. This went on for a very long time. A very. Long. Time. Meanwhile, the natives were growing restless. Her name got passed down the line, and everyone started trying to—er, encourage her, subjecting her to peer pressure in chant form: "Er-in! Er-in! Er-in!" It didn't work. Erin didn't go. Erin never went.

Some of us are Erin. We're standing on a platform overlooking a challenge in our life—a problem we need to face head-on, a change we need to make, a new chapter we need to embrace. It's time to jump in, to take the figurative leap. Jesus is waiting below us in the water (or *on* the water!) with arms outstretched. He is offering an encouraging smile and saying, "Come." But we stand frozen on the ledge, trapped in indecision. Analyzing the risks: the height of the waves, the strength of the wind, the depths of the water. And the longer we hesitate, the tighter fear grips us. We don't want to go back, but we are too afraid to go forward.

When It's Time for a "Come to Jesus"

We have a saying here in the South: "It's time for a Come to Jesus." Your kid tells a lie? Time to have a Come to Jesus. An addict gets a DUI? Time to have a Come to Jesus. Your boss says get it together or lose your job? Well, you just had a Come to Jesus with your boss, and you'd better go home and have a Come to Jesus *with Jesus* if you want to keep your job!

A Come to Jesus is a point in time when life stops for one fleeting *Matrix* moment: Time slows. Fog clears. Vision sharpens. Here in one standing-on-the-ledge moment, we have an opportunity to change. To confront ourselves, demons and all; to stare the truest, most sinful, ugliest parts of our sinful nature square in the face. To behold grace in all its beauty, held out for us even here in this dark moment, ready for the taking—and then to give our all to Jesus. To give *ourselves* to Jesus. To say, "Here I am, Lord. I surrender. Take me and change me. I'm Yours."

The Bible calls this repentance.

Some of us have *almost* had Come to Jesus moments. I remember several such moments, back in my early teen years, when I wasn't sure I wanted to do—or even *could* do—this Christianity thing. I had been studying the Bible on my own for a while, pondering the decision to become a Christian—to embrace the faith my parents had so lovingly passed on to me, to finally make it my own—but I was putting it off. I wasn't ready. I didn't really want to be ready. I kept going to church, kept going to youth group, kept reading my Bible every morning, but I had never gone all in. I was comfortably religious, and that was as far as I wanted it to go.

Several times I sat on my bed with my Bible open, feeling God's Word knocking on my heart, feeling a squirmy sensation in my gut, hearing a gentle voice prompting, "It's time, Elizabeth. Time to surrender. Time to let go and *go for it*"—but every time I panicked. Shut the Book and moved on with my life. Within a few hours, the moment always faded. The opening in my heart retracted.

For long months, pride, fear, complacency, and a host of other sins got the better of me. Every time I thought about giving my life to God, I heard worldly voices coo, "Come this way, Elizabeth. Happiness and peace aren't as expensive as God says. With us you can have fame, approval, success. An easy life with no sacrifices.

With us you can date anyone you want—who cares if he loves God as long as he's cute? With us your life can be all about you, only you, wonderful you. With us you can chuck your conscience out the window and never feel guilty again."

I felt darkness descending, a darkness so thick it covered the walls of my heart, sealing the gaps, closing me in. The door of my heart remained open to God—just a crack—but every time I let a Come to Jesus moment pass me by, I felt the door closing, the crack shrinking, till barely a sliver of light remained.

Cue Come to Jesus conversation with Jesus. One afternoon, prompted by a heart-to-heart talk with my mother, I lay facedown on the floor of my bedroom and begged God, "Please help me. I feel so hard. I know I need to give You my heart, and I'm afraid if I don't change now, my heart will harden forever. Please, God—I don't want to change, but *I want to want to*. So please help me go from there."

I sat on my bed and opened to Isaiah 65 and read these words for the first time—words God had spoken to His rebellious people when they, like me, were pushing Him away:

> *"I revealed myself to those who did not ask for me;*
> *I was found by those who did not seek me.*
> *To a nation that did not call on my name,*
> *I said, 'Here am I, here am I.'*
> *All day long I have held out my hands*
> *to an obstinate people,*
> *who walk in ways not good,*
> *pursuing their own imaginations—*
> *a people who continually provoke me*
> *to my very face. . .*
> *who say, 'Keep away; don't come near me,*
> *for I am too sacred for you!' "*

VERSES 1–3, 5

This was me. All my life God had revealed Himself to me. All my life He had held out His hands, inviting me to love and be loved: "Here I am, Elizabeth! Come, be close to Me!"

And this—finally, this—pierced my heart: The image of God standing before me, arms out, and me turning my back. Walking away. With a shock of clarity, I realized that Christianity wasn't a list of "to dos" and "to give ups." No, Christianity was a *relationship.* A choice to give myself wholly to the One who loved me and wanted my love in return. The One who kept seeking me, meeting my crossed arms with His open ones.

And in that moment, I surrendered. I got back down on my face on my floor again and wept my regret, my apology, my surrender.

The next day I stood in the waters of baptism and pronounced three powerful, sobering, and scary words, the words I had resisted for so long: "Jesus is Lord." I said them as slowly and forcefully as my teenage body could muster. I came to Jesus. I went under the water. I went all in.

Go Big

Peter seemed to live by the motto "Go big or go home." Either he was going big—walking on water—or he was going down. . .down in the proverbial blaze of glory, publicly cursing the name of the friend he loved. Peter's story—especially his struggles—can give hope to all of us as we seek to answer the call of Christ. Peter had quite a few of his own Come to Jesus moments:

Peter had to (literally) come to Jesus when the Lord said, "Come, follow me. . .and I will send you out to fish for people" (Mark 1:17). Peter had to leave his nets—leave his life—and go wherever Jesus went.

Peter had to come to Jesus after the miraculous catch of fish, a divine display so staggering that Peter cried, "Go away from me, Lord; I am a sinful man!" (Luke 5:1–11).

Peter had to come to Jesus when the Lord tried to wash his feet but Peter tried to push Him away—again Peter quailed in the face of his own unworthiness. He didn't want the grace.

Peter *should have* come to Jesus in the courtyard of the high priest the night before the crucifixion, but instead he "followed at a distance." And soon he cursed His name.

Peter had to come to Jesus—come *back* to Jesus—on the beach after the resurrection, when Jesus gently but pointedly reinstated him.

Truth? When I read Peter's story, I feel more hopeful about myself—my flaws, my feelings, my fears. . .my tendency to "pull an Erin" any time Jesus says, "Come." Maybe I can make it after all. Like Peter, I have followed Jesus with a lot of fear and even more tears. I didn't just "come to Jesus" the one time when I got baptized—I have had to come *back* to Jesus many times:

My freshman year in college, when the Christian boy I loved didn't love me back, and it was tempting to settle for someone who didn't love God with all his heart.

A few months into my marriage, when it was time to tackle some unhealthy emotional patterns that were hurting my new husband.

All day every day and all night every night when I endured a long season of infertility, and all my friends became mothers without me.

When God finally said yes and we went from no babies to three babies in less than three years (we call it the Turbo Family Plan, and no, you should not try this at home if you value your sanity, your sleep, and your savings account!), and we were so grateful we could hardly stand it but so exhausted we could hardly stand up.

When we lost a pregnancy at the same time we lost the place—and the people—we called home.

When people hurt people I love.

When we moved to a new city to plant a church, and all my ministry fears came howling to the surface.

When my literary agent called and said, "You got a deal to write a Christian book!". . .and I couldn't decide if I was trembling from excitement or from absolute God-picked-the-wrong-person terror.

When Jesus says, "Come," it's time to go. When Jesus says, "Come," it's time to go big, because when He calls, He wants our all.

Just listen to Jesus' challenging words describing what it means to follow Him (and take a deep breath—reading all of these at once feels a bit like trying to take a sip of water from a fire hydrant):

> *"Whoever wants to be my disciple must deny themselves and take up their cross daily and follow me. For whoever wants to save their life will lose it, but whoever loses their life for me will save it. What good is it for someone to gain the whole world, and yet lose or forfeit their very self? Whoever is ashamed of me and my words, the Son of Man will be ashamed of them when he comes in his glory and in the glory of the Father and of the holy angels."*
>
> LUKE 9:23–26

> *As they were walking along the road, a man said to him, "I will follow you wherever you go."*
>
> *Jesus replied, "Foxes have dens and birds have nests, but the Son of Man has no place to lay his head."*
>
> *He said to another man, "Follow me."*
>
> *But he replied, "Lord, first let me go and bury my father."*
>
> *Jesus said to him, "Let the dead bury their own dead, but you go and proclaim the kingdom of God."*
>
> *Still another said, "I will follow you, Lord; but first let me go back and say goodbye to my family."*
>
> *Jesus replied, "No one who puts a hand to the plow and looks back is fit for service in the kingdom of God."*
>
> LUKE 9:57–62

"If you want to be my disciple, you must, by comparison, hate everyone else—your father and mother, wife and children, brothers and sisters—yes, even your own life. Otherwise, you cannot be my disciple. And if you do not carry your own cross and follow me, you cannot be my disciple."

Luke 14:26–27 nlt

It's an unflinching standard. Coming to Jesus costs everything: relationships, possessions, talents. Jesus calls us to put Him first. And not just first—He wants to be first, last, and everything in between. He wants to *be* our life. As Paul put it, "Christ. . .is your life" (Colossians 3:4).

Okay, I know. Some of you are hyperventilating right now. Pass me the paper bag when you're done with it! I have been a disciple of Jesus for more than twenty-five years, but every time I read those passages, they still cut me. They still intimidate me. Yes, the price of following Jesus is scary, overwhelming, and *expensive*, but it would be wrong for us to water down His call to make it easier or more palatable. As my preacher father likes to say, "The pearl of great price never goes on sale"—and it's worth every penny.

When You Can't Negotiate

If I were Peter in that boat that night, I might have been tempted to say, "You know, Jesus, I am excited about the opportunity to walk on water with You. Truly, I am. But couldn't You do that trick where You calm the wind and waves first? You know, the miracle You did that time when You were napping on the boat and we were all freaking out? (Not our finest hour, I know.) I think the walk would be so much more enjoyable for both of us if the water were calm, don't You? Not to mention a little less scary and dangerous? Don't You think the whole water-walking concept is radical enough without the complication of the crazy waves?"

Anybody else like to negotiate with God like this? Manipulate circumstances to remove as much risk and discomfort as possible?

But when I—can I say we?—try to negotiate with God like this, how much we miss! We miss the excitement of adventure, the exhilaration of trust, the mind-blowing miracle of "This is all God and no me—this could only happen with Him."

Having read the difficult passages, having evaluated the cost, let us also remember: Jesus loves us and gives us grace when we fall short. When He calls us to come, He doesn't just challenge us; He also comforts us. Walks alongside us. Protects us. Heals us. He promises, "Come to Me, all you who are weary, and I will give you rest. My yoke is easy and My burden is light" (see Matthew 11:28–30). And He says, "I have come that they may have life, and have it to the full" (John 10:10). Somehow the difficult things and the comforting things are all true—equally true—at the same time. This is one of the deep mysteries of our faith. A beautiful paradox.

When I struggle with feeling overwhelmed and inadequate in the face of Jesus' high expectations, I often think about how I feel when I witness new couples making their marriage vows. Is it just me, or have marriage vows become increasingly elaborate in recent years? As if it weren't tough enough to promise to love, honor, and cherish one another "for richer, for poorer, in sickness and in health, till God by death shall separate us," now couples make detailed personal vows involving weekly date nights, household chores, and even sports-watching habits! When I'm sitting in the audience witnessing wedding vows, here's a peek into my tortured internal dialogue:

The bride says something like: "I, the lovestruck bride, take thee, my equally lovestruck groom, to be my wedded husband. I promise to worship the ground you walk on every day and never let our romance fade the teeniest, tiniest bit. I promise to sit happily on the couch watching your favorite team play because I know how important it is to you, and if it's important to you, it's important to me. I promise to cook your favorite foods, and if you'll do the dishes I'll do the laundry (as long as you help me fold). I promise never to grow tired of our relationship, never to take you for granted, never to stop putting you first before myself forever and ever, every day, with every beat of my heart, amen."

Me to myself, looking down at my forty-year-old fingers, interlaced with forty-year-old Kevin's, remembering our eighteen marital years together: *Well, I must be a bad wife. Because as much as I still adore Kevin, there have been days when I haven't worshipped the ground he walks on. (Especially when that ground is covered in his balled-up dirty socks that I keep begging him to put in the laundry basket.) He figured out pretty quickly that I don't care about football at all unless he himself is playing in the game (which he hasn't done for fifteen years). And his favorite foods are all filled with dairy, which makes him snore, so I don't cook those nearly as often as he wants me to.*

By now I am squirming in my seat, my hand growing sweaty in Kevin's: *Some days I have taken him for granted. Some days I have given in to bad moods and PMS. Some days I have been selfish and put myself before him. I AM A TERRIBLE WIFE.*

When I listen to the detailed vows, the extravagant love, the over-the-top promises, I start feeling overwhelmed. Guilty. Insecure. But here's the funny thing: I have a happy marriage. Like, way-above-average happy. We aren't perfect, but we laugh way more than we argue. We work well together. We disagree sometimes, but we almost always keep conflict low-key and fair-minded. Kevin eats less dairy than he'd like, but he is well fed. Even though I don't watch football with him as often as he wants me to—I've given up even pretending to like it—we still love hanging out together. We love being married to each other—dirty socks on the floor, four-kid chaos, and you-know-ice-cream-makes-you-snore-so-why-are-you-being-selfish-and-eating-it "discussions" and all.

Let's not overthink our Christianity any more than we overthink our commitments in marriage. We have to count the cost, yes; we're called to go all in, yes, but let's remember: We get married because we're in love. We get married because we have found our favorite person. We are willing to do the hard stuff because all the good stuff is *so totally worth it*. It's the same with Christianity. We go all in for Jesus because we love Him. We go all in for Jesus because He is the greatest person ever in the history of people. We go all in for Jesus because He went all in for us first. We go all in for Jesus because He shows us how we were meant to live, who we were meant to be.

As Jesus said, "The kingdom of heaven is like treasure hidden in a field. When a man found it, he hid it again, and then *in his joy* went and sold all he had and bought that field" (Matthew 13:44, emphasis added). We sell everything we have because we have found something infinitely more valuable. We go all in, and when we really understand what we've found, it's all joy.

All In at Every Age

I went all in for Jesus when I was fourteen. And "all in" for Jesus at fourteen looked a lot different than going all in for Jesus at forty. Forty-year-old Elizabeth has to make choices fourteen-year-old Elizabeth couldn't even fathom. I face a host of new fears, new weaknesses, new choices. My life has grown fuller, my schedule crazier, my responsibilities weightier. At every new stage of life, I have to reignite my heart and recommit my love, making Jesus the Lord of my life all over again. And it's not over yet—going all in for Jesus will look different when I am fifty. . .or sixty. . .or seventy. . .as many years as God gifts me. I'll have to surrender new things, surrender the new (older!) me.

Maybe you have gone all in for Jesus in the past, but as life has changed, you also have changed; you have taken some steps back. What would it look like if you went all in for Jesus now? At *this* stage of your life? Now as a college student. . .a spouse. . .an employee. . .a divorcée. . .a parent. . .a grandparent? Maybe you went all in once upon a time, but if you jumped overboard today, what would that mean?

- Would you choose a college for spiritual reasons

instead of solely academic ones? A career for spiritual reasons instead of financial ones?

- Would you look for a different kind of person to date?
- Would you let go of bitterness and finally forgive?
- Would you open up to Christian friends about weakness and sin, inviting help?
- Would you stand up for God's ways in a world that pressures us to blend in and water down?
- Would you simplify your schedule, removing the fluff, so you could devote more time to God and to His people?
- Would you offer your best talent, your best work, to God—instead of the world?
- Would you learn how to study the Bible with your neighbors?

Yes, the older we get the more we have to lose. Yes, we know more than we wish we did about the ways of the world, the pain in the world. But no matter our age or stage of life, the *same Jesus* is out there waiting for us. The *same Jesus* is ready to catch us if the wind and waves get the better of us. He is just as faithful, just as trustworthy, just as powerful now as He was when we first tried our hands—or rather our feet—at water-walking.

When Jesus Says, "Come"

When Jesus says, "Come," we have to get out of our safe, comfortable boat with its life rafts and ropes, and we have to walk on water. We have to go out where it's dangerous. Out where no one but Jesus can help us walk. Out where we cannot survive on our own. Out where other believers might not dare to go. And if we don't want to sink, we have to take our eyes off the wind and the waves and fix them on Jesus.

Jesus calls us all, no matter where we are: New to faith, pondering a jump. Settled in Christ, needing a push. Mature in Christ, fighting weariness. At every stage, God calls us forward. At every age, Jesus says, "Come." He stands before us, arms wide, promising that if we jump—when we jump—though the waves may be wild, our feet will stand firm.

Let's Go Deeper. . .

For Further Study
Read Matthew 11:28–30 and reread Matthew 13:44–46. How can these scriptures help us to rise to the challenging call of discipleship—and to embrace it with joy?

Journal Prompt
1. Is it time for a Come to Jesus in a certain area of your life? What is that area, and what is Jesus asking you to do?
2. What scares you most about giving your all to Jesus? About going overboard for Him?
3. What would your life look like if you went all in for Jesus today?

Prayer Prompt
You, God, are my God,
        earnestly I seek you;
I thirst for you,
        my whole being longs for you,
in a dry and parched land
        where there is no water. . . .
Because your love is better than life,
        my lips will glorify you.
Psalm 63:1, 3

5
When God Changes
Your Plans

The Story of Mary the
Mother of Jesus, Part 1

Based on Luke 1:26–38 and Psalm 16

Mary's fingers work the loom, the threads in white and gold. As she works, she hums—a wedding song, the song her family will sing during the wedding week as they walk her through the streets to Joseph's house. The night their marriage is confirmed. The thought makes her smile, then flush. Her fingers lose the rhythm. Long moments she sits, no longer seeing thread, loom, or room— she sees her parents, smiling and proud. Her childhood friends, happy and a little envious. Joseph, his dark eyes mysterious. The eyes she has known since childhood—first as family friend, now as. . .betrothed. Husband.

Husband. She rolls the word around inside, tasting its newness. *Wife.* A little laugh escapes. Who is she, to have been given such a man, such a life? All her girlhood dreams, coming true so soon. Still laughing to herself, she shuts her eyes and prays: "Lord, You alone are my portion and my cup; You make my lot secure. The boundary lines have fallen for me in pleasant places; surely I have a delightful inheritance" (Psalm 16:5–6).

A noise at the door startles her—she reaches quickly for the loom, waiting for Mother's disapproving words to issue from the doorway: "Daydreaming is for girls, not for wives," she will say. "When you run your own home, you cannot afford the luxury of these childish ways, all this sitting and singing and drifting off."

But the voice does not come. Mary spins around on her stool and gasps.

A man stands in the doorway. A large man, muscular, intimidating, and—it embarrasses her to think it—beautiful. He smiles, and there is something in the smile—something ageless, something powerful, something *knowing*. His eyes lock on hers and she squirms, feeling that he sees to the depths of her. Reads her thoughts. Sees her heart.

She skips her eyes away. Fear steals her voice, traps her on the stool. This man should not be here, alone in a room with her. He should not be looking at her. She should not be looking at him. She should scream, she should run, she should—

"Greetings, you who are highly favored," the man rumbles, inclining his head. "The Lord is with you."

"I— Sorry, what? Do I know you?" Mary's eyes dart around the room, seeking a way out, wishing someone would come—Father, Mother, her brothers, Joseph—anyone.

"Don't be afraid, Mary." He raises his hands. Her stomach lurches in fear. *What is he doing?* A gust of impossible wind blows in the room, smelling of—flowers? She breathes deeper. Lavender, her favorite. The scent soothes her even as a chill walks down her spine. She knows who he is, what he is. She doesn't know how she knows, exactly—*Well, the perfumed wind blowing indoors might be a hint*—but she knows.

Quiet words pass slowly through her dry lips. "So you're a–an—"

The man cocks his head sideways; his narrowed eyes hint at humor. "I believe the word you're looking for is—"

"Angel," Mary whispers. "Messenger." The room shimmers and spins.

He leans in close and whispers, "You should breathe."

Deeply she breathes in the calming scent.

The angel bows. "Gabriel," he says. "At your service."

Her hands tremble, and she clamps them together in her lap.

"Have I done someth–" she starts, in a voice hardly more than a whisper. Mother's voice rebukes her in her mind, cuts short her sentence: *"A wife stays quiet. Never question a man."* She thinks for a moment. *But he's NOT a man, Mother. Not exactly. . . And I am arguing with my mother and she's not even here.* Mary chokes down a noise that would have turned into a laugh under less terrifying circumstances.

With a gentle smile Gabriel repeats, "Don't be afraid, Mary; you have found favor with God."

The words hit her ears but not her mind. "Favor? With. . .God?"

A smile curls at the corner of Gabriel's mouth. "Favor is a *good* thing, Mary."

"Ah. Right." She accidentally gives him a small smile of relief, then, horrified, drops the smile and her eyes—*Are women allowed to smile at angels and look them in the eye? Is anyone? Oh, why isn't someone here to speak for me?*

The man stands tall; his voice is confident, musical: "You will conceive and give birth to a son, and you are to call him Jesus. He will be great and will be called the Son of the Most High. The Lord God will give him the throne of his father David, and he will reign over Jacob's descendants forever; his kingdom will never end."

Mary blinks at him. One minute, two minutes, three. Her mind grasps at the words, repeating them, slowing them down, trying to put them in an order that makes sense.

"I'm sorry—did you say 'give birth to a son'? As in"—she mimes the shape of a pregnant belly, realizing too late how inappropriate the gesture must be. Fire fills her cheeks.

The man nods with a large grin, showing two rows of perfect white teeth. Mary's hands fly up to cover her mouth. The words spin through her mind, faster and faster, over and over. *Birth to a son. Son of the Most High. Throne of David.* She falls off the stool, onto her knees.

The angel stands silent and unmoving, as if waiting for

something. Or giving her time.

Questions war within her: *Ask him why me. Ask him if he came to the right house. Ask him— No!* Clenching her fists, she cuts short the words. *Gabriel speaks truth—you know he does.* Her brain rapidly tries to rearrange all she had planned, all she had thought her life would hold—proper wedding, normal kids, quiet life—but none of it fits, none of it works in this new future Gabriel has described. At last she takes a full breath and wipes clean her thoughts. *That life is over. That plan is over. You only need to know what God would have you do next. How to obey.*

At last she looks up. Again she dares to meet the burning eyes, the deep-seeing gaze, and asks, "How will this be, since I am"— she gestures to herself, stumbling over the word—"a virgin?" Her cheeks burn again.

The angel tosses his head back and chuckles for a moment. "Now that's a good question, Mary." Crooking a finger, he indicates that she should stand.

With shaking knees she stands, placing one hand on the stool for support.

He bends a confidential smile down on her. "Between you and me, the last time I gave news of a miraculous birth to a mortal, he asked a stupid question—he doubted the truth of my words—and I had to mute him for the duration of the pregnancy. I can't tell you how happy I am you didn't do the same."

Mary offers him a wobbly smile. Almost manages a laugh.

Gabriel stands tall, grows serious once more. "The Holy Spirit will come on you, and the power of the Most High will overshadow you. So the holy one to be born will be called the Son of God. Even Elizabeth your relative is going to have a child in her old age"—at this Mary claps her hands over her mouth, tears of surprise and joy stinging her eyes—"and she who was said to be unable to conceive is in her sixth month." Gabriel beams down at her. "For no word from God will ever fail."

Mary's thoughts fold inward, shuffling through images: Her

beloved relative Elizabeth, so sad for so long, cradling a child at last. Mary's own small frame swollen with child. The Holy Spirit coming upon her—*What does that even mean? What will it look like, and what will it feel like?* Joseph's expression, her parents' expressions, when she tells them the news. At this she pauses, gut clenching. *The One who will help me conceive will also help me survive. Why would He go to all this trouble only to fail me in the details?*

She draws a long breath, standing as tall as she can. "I am the Lord's servant. May it be to me as you have said."

With another gust of wind, the angel disappears. Mary stands shaking in an empty room, seeing all the familiar things as if for the first time. Old things, new eyes. Everything the same, but everything changed.

You have never failed me, Lord—my life is in Your hands. She claps her hands to her mouth, holding in a shout, a cry, a laugh. *A baby! I'm going to have a baby!*

∞

In a single moment, Mary's entire life turned upside down, inside out, and every other way a life can turn. What an emotional whirlwind: excitement and fear, gratitude and confusion, wonder and worry. So much unknown.

In one day Mary went from a girl with a normal life plan—a plan she had likely dreamed about since girlhood, a plan that was sure to win the approval of her community (maybe even the envy of a few girlfriends)—to a young woman pregnant under suspicious circumstances. Her integrity and purity would now be called into question; her marriage and future were now at risk.

We catch a hint of the controversy surrounding Mary's pregnancy when we read Joseph's reaction: "Because Joseph her husband was faithful to the law, and yet did not want to expose her to public disgrace, he had in mind to divorce her quietly" (Matthew 1:19). How easy it is to read past all the drama and pain packed into that line! Considering the customs of the day, it is doubtful

Mary met with Joseph in person to break the news of her pregnancy; perhaps they communicated through messengers: Mary's father, Joseph's brother.

If Mary and Joseph were to have their conversation face-to-face in a more modern setting, I imagine it going something like this:

Mary: "Joseph, I have something to tell you."

Joseph (*mouth twitching*): "Your mother wants to invite more people to the wedding?"

Mary (*fiddling with shawl in her lap*): "Not exactly."

Joseph (*with a mischievous grin*): "You want to move the wedding date up because you can't stand waiting another day to be my wife?"

Mary (*trying to mirror his smile*): "Sort of."

Joseph (*with mock horror*): "Sort of? You only *sort of* can't wait to be my wife? I am offended!"

Mary (*trying—failing—to laugh*): "No, I—well, it's just, some things have. . .changed."

Joseph (*smile faltering*): "Changed? What do you mean, *changed*? Mary, you're scaring me. What's wrong?" (*He pauses.*) "Your father hasn't changed his mind, has he?"

Mary shakes her head.

Joseph: "You aren't having. . .doubts?"

Mary (*managing a smile*): "No, silly."

Joseph (*with an exaggerated sigh*): "Okay."

Mary: "I've practiced this a thousand times, and there's no easy way to say it, so. . .I'll just say it. Joseph, I—" (*She shuts her eyes and takes a deep breath.*) "I'm pregnant."

Long silence.

Joseph (*color draining from his face*): "Please tell me you're joking." (*He takes a step back, already distancing himself.*)

Mary (*shaking her head, holding out a hand as if to pull him close, to make him stay*): "No, I'm not joking. I—I had a visit from an angel. Gabriel."

Joseph: "An *angel*? You can't be serious. What kind of fool do you take me for, Mary?"

Mary (*fighting to speak through tears*): "Please, please let me finish." (*Words tumble quickly: the angel, the promise, the pregnancy.*)

Joseph (*listens quietly, his face painted red*): "At least you could tell me the truth, Mary. If you didn't want me—if you loved someone else. . ."

Mary (*sobbing now, hardly able to squeeze words through her strangled throat*): "No, please, Joseph—"

Joseph (*holding up a hand to cut her short, avoiding her eyes; his tone flat and empty, strangely defeated*): "I'll do it quietly, the divorce. I won't hand you over to the Pharisees with their cruelty and stones. You should go—go stay with someone before you. . .before it's obvious."

Joseph (*turning away, shaking his head*): "Goodbye, Mary. I never saw this coming."

Mary (*whispering*): "Neither did I."

We don't know exactly how Mary delivered the news to Joseph, but we do know she couldn't convince him of her innocence. God had to intervene, sending an angel to Joseph to corroborate Mary's story. But consider this: As far as we know, Joseph was the only person in Mary's life who got a visit from an angel. It seems everyone else—Mary's mother, father, siblings, and friends—had to take Mary at her word: "So I had a visit from an angel, and I'm still a virgin, but I'm pregnant by the Holy Spirit with the Son of God. . . ." *Riiiight.*

What were Mary's relationships like from this time forward? Did she live the rest of her life with a stain on her reputation? Did Joseph's reputation also suffer? Was the wedding ceremony subdued, tainted by scandal? Did other women shun Mary at the well for years afterward? We don't know all that, but we do know that Mary's life was never the same.

Has God ever changed your life plan? Pushed you to go in a new and unexpected direction? A direction you might not have chosen for yourself?

Here's how it usually goes when God hands me a life change I hadn't anticipated:

God: So guess what? Some things are about to change in your life. It's time to go in a new direction. It's time for something different.

Me (*crazy-eyed and squeaky-voiced*): Different? What do you mean, different? As long as *different* means "basically the exact same way life has been," then that's totally fine. I'm completely up for it. I trust You.

Long, quiet pause. God raises an eyebrow, looking vaguely amused.

Me (*breathing way too fast*): Also, as long as *different* means "not too difficult or uncomfortable," then that's fine. I trust you.

Another long pause. God crosses His arms and waits.

Me (*riffling through cabinets, searching for a paper bag*): Sorry, one more thing. As long as *different* means "exactly what I had planned for my life, only a slightly happier and more successful plan than I had dared to dream," then that's fine. I trust You.

God (*burying His face in His hands as I hyperventilate into a bag*): Oh, Elizabeth, where do I even start with you?

Sometimes God says, "Go," and then points us to a place we never imagined. Never wanted. While most of us won't receive an angelic visit announcing our next life surprise, we all experience change: moves, promotions, job loss, marriage, infertility, pregnancy, health problems, conflict, financial struggle. . .and the list goes on. Even when our life changes come from a "human," earthbound source, we can be sure that God is not unaware—or uninvolved in our journey.

How can we navigate changes in our plans with our joy, peace, and sense of humor intact? How can we weather times of transition without doubting God, doubting ourselves, or—how do we say this diplomatically—turning into useless puddles of self-pitying tears on the floor? (Anyone else ever done this? Just me? Oh. Well then, this next part is just for me.) Let's break this down as practically as we can.

1. Ask respectful questions.

Mary didn't just silently accept the news—she asked a respectful question to clarify her expectations and her role: "How will this be, since I am a virgin?" Considering the fertility technology of the day, it was a valid question!

But think about all the questions Mary could have asked Gabriel:

"Why me?"

"Will you make sure everyone knows I haven't done anything wrong?"

"Can you talk me through exactly who this boy is going to be when He grows up?"

"Are you sure I won't be stoned for this? And can I get that guaranteed in writing?"

But faithful Mary asks none of those questions. She doesn't ask for favors or assurances of safety and happiness—she just asks for greater understanding. And Gabriel is happy to give it. Mary's example shows us that it's okay to ask God, "Hey, Father, how is this going to go? I see where You are pointing me—now how do I get there?"

When God hands us change, although it is not necessarily sinful to ask why, nor is it wrong to take the time we need to process the change (see the Psalms for examples of prayers like this),

Mary's example points us to the place of faith where we eventually want to arrive.

2. Keep talking to God.

Sometimes we think being "surrendered" to God's will means we should just swallow our questions and deal with it. But as in any relationship, when we stuff our true feelings, resentment builds.

If you study the way our spiritual ancestors related to our heavenly Father, a pattern emerges: they were not afraid to bring real feelings—even hard questions—to God. Most were careful to do so respectfully, with reverence and submission, acknowledging God's sovereignty and right to choose *for* them. . .but still, they had raw, heartfelt conversations with Him.

Let's leave Mary's story for a moment to drop in on someone who handled a life change with a bit more panic. In a single day, the prophet Elijah goes from conquering the spiritual mountaintop to running for the hills. (I'm not writing metaphorically here—this is literally what happened!) After an epic mountaintop showdown with—and bloodstained victory over—the enemies of God, four hundred prophets of Baal, Elijah becomes a target of the evil queen Jezebel. Although Elijah did not cower before four hundred prophets, now a single queen's wrath triggers his fear. He ends up running away, hiding in a cave, and God comes looking for him. The dialogue here is taken word for word from the Bible:

God: What are you doing here, Elijah?
Elijah: I have been very zealous for the Lord God Almighty.
The Israelites have rejected your covenant, torn down your altars, and put your prophets to death with the sword. I am the only one left, and now they are trying to kill me too.

Time out. Do you hear the honesty here? Elijah lays out the facts and then ends with an emotional truth: he feels like the only faithful one left. Not only is he afraid; he is feeling sorry for himself. And he is bold enough to admit this to God. *Okay, time in.*

God: *Go back the way you came*, and go to the Desert of Damascus. When you get there, anoint Hazael king over Aram. Also, anoint Jehu son of Nimshi king over Israel, and anoint Elisha son of Shaphat from Abel Meholah to succeed you as prophet. . . . Yet I reserve seven thousand in Israel—all whose knees have not bowed down to Baal and whose mouths have not kissed him. *(The dialogue here is taken directly from 1 Kings 19:13–18, with emphasis added. You can read the whole story in 1 Kings 18 and 19 if you want to better understand the situation.)*

Did you catch that? God sends Elijah back. Back to the situation he was running away from. Back with a greater sense of His protective presence. Back with instructions and a solution: "Anoint kings and appoint a successor so you don't feel so alone." Back with a better understanding of reality: "By the way, buddy, you're not alone. I've got seven thousand other people who are also faithful to Me."

What an interaction! This single conversation depicts the kindness *and* firmness of God, how the two go hand in hand. First God encouraged Elijah. Then He equipped Elijah, providing help for the situation he was in, including a fellow prophet to share his burdens. And then God said, "Go." Actually, God said, "Go back." Go back into spiritual battle once more.

If you are in a situation that has you running for the hills, hiding in caves, and trembling in fear, talk to God about it. Ask for His presence, His help, and His guidance. Ask to see Him through the darkness. If your eyes are too dim and the darkness too thick for you to see, ask to *feel* Him by your side. Ask Him to take your hand and guide you to the light.

3. Read scriptures that remind you how God feels about you. Read them until you believe them. (This might take awhile.)

My first reaction when life changes—particularly when it changes in an undesirable way—is to assume the worst about my relationship with God. To assume that He is angry with me or punishing me or even—please let me not get struck by lightning for confessing this awful truth—out to get me.

In this book we are exploring the lives of ten people whom God called. None of them had easy lives, but never would we think, *God made Mary get pregnant because He didn't love her. He did it to be mean and ruin her life.*

No! Because we have access to years' worth of Mary's life story, we are able to view this one moment from a big-picture perspective. We can see that as difficult as this change was for a short time, in the end it was a great honor. A sign of God's confidence and approval. A gift—the greatest of her life. We know that God remained faithful, that He saw Mary through all the difficulties that came along with being the mother of Jesus.

But when it comes to our own lives, our own sudden changes, we think, *Yeah, well, you can't compare Mary's life to mine. There is no big-picture grand plan for my life. God hasn't handpicked me to raise His Son because of my spiritual awesomeness. I'm just going through a hard time for no reason.*

Here are a few scriptures that remind me of God's unwavering love even through big change:

> *"Though the mountains be shaken*
> *and the hills be removed,*
> *yet my unfailing love for you will not be shaken*
> *nor my covenant of peace be removed,"*
> *says the* Lord, *who has compassion on you.*
> Isaiah 54:10

We think of mountains as permanent things, huge and unshakable. But sometimes even mountains fall. And when mountains in our lives are shaken—marriage, family, health, everything that makes us who we are—God's love remains. When all else changes, when it seems the whole world is falling apart, God's love never changes. God's love never fails.

> *The eyes of the LORD are on the righteous,*
> *and his ears are attentive to their cry. . . .*
> *The righteous cry out, and the LORD hears them;*
> *he delivers them from all their troubles.*
> *The LORD is close to the brokenhearted*
> *and saves those who are crushed in spirit.*
> *The righteous person may have many troubles,*
> *but the LORD delivers him from them all.*
>
> PSALM 34:15, 17–19

Being righteous doesn't mean we don't face troubles. In fact, we may face *many*. But no trouble is bigger than our God, no failure is beyond redemption, and great heartache draws Him near. He doesn't always make our troubles go away—but in *His* own way He sees us through.

And lest we think these scriptures are just for "God's people" in general, and not for you and me in particular, remember these precious words from Mary's son Jesus—He who knew the mind and heart of God better than anyone: "Are not five sparrows sold for two pennies? Yet not one of them is forgotten by God. Indeed, the very hairs of your head are all numbered. Don't be afraid; you are worth more than many sparrows" (Luke 12:6–7).

4. Remember whose opinion matters.
After Gabriel's visit, Mary sings this prayer to God:

"My soul glorifies the Lord
and my spirit rejoices in God my Savior,
for he has been mindful
of the humble state of his servant.
From now on all generations will call me blessed,
for the Mighty One has done great things for me—
holy is his name."

Luke 1:46–49

I doubt many of Mary's neighbors are calling her "blessed" —"promiscuous," "dishonest," and "crazy" are likelier adjectives— but Mary chooses to see the situation (and herself) through God's eyes. Where the world cries scandal, Mary claims honor. Some people will eventually call Mary blessed, but for now she recognizes God's opinion as the only one that matters. She has God's approval, and that is enough.

5. Seek joy in the small moments, peace in the big picture.

Mary celebrates her new role, confident that the God who has brought this change into her life will also guide her through all the change to come: "From now on all generations will call me blessed." Mary finds the faith to look past her temporary difficulties to adopt a heavenly viewpoint. She finds the faith to look ahead (far ahead) to what her "unplanned pregnancy" will mean not just for her own life—*her* marriage, *her* relationships, *her* reputation—but also what it will mean for the generations to come, all the people (you! me! our children!) who will one day benefit.

And this perspective allows Mary to embrace her role—to enjoy her role—as Jesus grows. We see her treasuring precious, if somewhat bewildering, moments with her unusual son. When an old man takes eight-day-old Jesus into his arms and prophesies over His future, Mary and Joseph marvel (Luke 2:33). When preteen Jesus gives his parents a near heart attack by disappearing for three days (they find Him in the temple hanging out with the rabbis), Mary "treasure[s] all these things in her heart" (Luke 2:51). She doesn't understand it all, can't grasp exactly who Jesus is meant to be, but even so she savors the experience of being His mother. Stores it up inside as God-gifted treasure.

6. Don't mistake "easy" for "godly."
Mary's miracle child was born so that He might serve for a time but then suffer and die. Just because something is difficult, controversial, or painful doesn't mean it is outside the will of God. Few of us would choose suffering for ourselves, but God's big-picture plan sometimes involves injustice and pain. His path for us is often more difficult than the one we would choose for ourselves.

When my husband and I moved to North Carolina to plant a new church, the first few years were far from the glorious "Look how fast our church grew and how many people we brought to the Lord" victory story we had hoped to have. The first few years were mostly exhausting. Confusing. Lonely. We were insecure, homesick, and—thanks to mold in our old rental house—chronically sick. I can't tell you how often Satan whispered, "Have you made a mistake? Is this not what God wanted you to do?"

But time and again, my way-more-faithful-and-God-focused-than-me husband reminded me, "*Difficult* doesn't mean *wrong.*" God has shown His faithfulness, wisdom, and kindness to us through every difficulty. The hardships have proven to be opportunities for growth, even vehicles for blessing.

After five years, our little church is still chugging along and happily growing—still loving each other, flaws and all; still reaching out to our community, sharing God's love the best we know how. Our marriage is strong, our children flourishing. (And as of this year, praise the sweet Lord in heaven, we finally have family in town—and that changes everything.)

7. Give your heart quickly to new places and people.
If I had been in Mary's shoes, poor Gabriel would have had to

hang around for a week or so answering a million questions, helping me process all the *feelings*. (And now we know why God didn't pick me. . . .)

How much energy and time—how much *life*—do we waste fighting change that has already happened? The die is cast, the deed is done, but like stubborn children we throw ourselves on the floor, kicking and wailing, "It's not fair! I didn't ask for this! My life might have been so different!" Fair or not, the change has happened. And we can't go forward if we're pouting in a corner or throwing tantrums on the floor. (*Ahem*. I may or may not have done this. I may or may not have done this a lot of times. And like Forrest Gump, "That's all I have to say about that.")

We may not get to choose when or how life changes, but we do get to choose how we respond. Practically speaking, "what might have been" is a waste of time. A waste of life. Because *what might have been* can never be—it is fantasy. As Solomon wisely tells us, "Whoever watches the wind will not plant; whoever looks at the clouds will not reap" (Ecclesiastes 11:4). If we sit around wind-watching—dreaming about the "good old days," wishing our lives away—we will never plant seeds in our new lives; if we never plant seeds, we can never reap joy. Let us choose to open our hearts to new situations. Find home in new places. Give our hearts to new people. When circumstances change, let us give God a chance to reveal His goodness, His wisdom, and His faithfulness no matter where we go.

When Life Hands You Grief

None of us plan to suffer. None of us plan to grieve. To fail at something we longed to achieve. To remain single forever and ever. To become single again after marriage. To face infertility. To battle chronic illness, endless pain. To feel crippled by anxiety or depression. To watch a beloved child go astray. To lose people we love before their time.

Losses like these often happen out of our control and out of the blue. One day life is dandy, we're happy and free, and then—*wham*—life turns on us. (And if we're honest, in the dark, secret corners of our hearts, we may even feel that *God Himself* has turned on us.)

There is great courage in facing grief. In starting over. In learning to live again, to love again, after great loss.

Lori didn't just have a marriage; she had a love affair. Married at twenty-four, she spent thirty-six happy years walking through life hand in hand with her husband Brad. Together they raised three beautiful children who grew up to love the Lord just as they did. Life wasn't perfect, but it was together, and *together* made everything better. And then one day Brad, a marathon runner and triathlete, went out for a run. As he shut the door, he smiled and said, "I won't be gone long."

But he was gone forever. Gone to a heart attack no one saw coming.

Death's immediate aftermath was a whirlwind of busyness, a welcome distraction: Planning the funeral. Hosting the family. Dealing with insurance.

But then everyone trickled out of town, back to their homes. One morning Lori woke up to an empty house for the first time. A house without kids, a house without Brad. So many small griefs she faced that first morning alone: Waking up to a too-quiet house. Trying not to notice the empty half of the bed. Making half a pot of coffee, because no one was there to drink the other half.

And soon it was time for her first day back at school teaching—again, so many fresh wounds: Getting dressed for work without Brad to offer sweet compliments. Heading out the door with no one to kiss good-bye.

But Lori was determined. She sat with God that morning and tearfully promised Him—promised herself—"I may feel like I have rocks in my pocket, but today I am going to be brave, giving, and even joyful. I am going to let people see the joy of the Lord. And I'm not going to hide my grief. If I need to cry, I'll cry, and that's okay."

That first morning, she walked into her classroom and stood in front of a roomful of insecure children staring up at her with questions in their eyes. She told them, "As some of you know, my husband died a few weeks ago. There may be some days when you see me crying, and that just means I'm having a hard day, but I will be okay."

Sure enough, Lori cried some days. And on those days her students swarmed her with hugs. One little boy would come up to her unprompted about once a week, wrap his arms around her waist, tip his head back, and say, "It's gonna be okay, Mrs. Bynum. Everything's gonna be okay." And through little-boy hugs she felt the arms of the Lord; in lisped, quiet words she heard the voice of the Lord. In time she cried less and smiled more. As the days passed she learned to live again. A different life without the love of her life, but still, somehow—with God—a life worth living.

The Lord's Servant

Mary's life went sideways in a single day. Her whole life, changed. Her entire identity, transformed. She didn't have it all figured out. Didn't get all her questions answered. Didn't grasp the full picture. Down the road, as we will explore in chapter 7, there were times when Mary got confused. Times when she misunderstood her son and resisted His role.

But here at the beginning, with life in upheaval, Mary trusted that God was with her. That He was in the change. That He held her life in His capable hands. She closes her encounter with Gabriel by saying, "I am the Lord's servant. May it be to me as you have said."

I am the Lord's servant. A more literal—and, if we're honest, a more uncomfortable—translation of Mary's words would be, "I am the Lord's slave." Five simple words, a huge life lesson: Mary understood that her individual life was part of God's big-picture plan. That God's agenda was more important than hers.

Being the Lord's servant means the Lord is in charge. Mary understood what Proverbs tells us: "Many are the plans in a person's heart, but it is the LORD's purpose that prevails" (Proverbs 19:21). It takes true humility and total surrender to give control to God. To say, "You know better than I do." Or, in the words of Mary's son some thirty years later: "Yet not as I will, but as You will."

Sometimes God says, "Go," and His destination surprises us. When God changes our direction midjourney, let's trust Him with Mary's kind of quiet courage. When questions go unanswered and our future looks cloudy, let us remain confident in God's kindness. When life hands us grief, let us face it with Mary's resilience. When God brings change, let us find the faith to say, "I am the Lord's servant."

Let's Go Deeper. . .

For Further Study
Mary wasn't the only one who received a life-changing visit from the angel Gabriel. For a fun study, contrast Mary's response with her relative Zechariah's. Mary's story is found in Matthew 1:18–2:23 and Luke 1:26–56; Zechariah's is in Luke 1:5–25, 57–80.

Journal Prompt
1. What feelings, fears, and faith questions do you face when life changes unexpectedly?
2. Can you think of a time when God has seen you through an unanticipated change? How specifically did He provide for your needs (physical, spiritual, emotional, relational)?

Prayer Prompt
The LORD foils the plans of the nations;
*   he thwarts the purposes of the peoples.*
But the plans of the LORD stand firm forever,
*   the purposes of his heart through all generations.*
PSALM 33:10–11

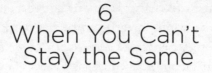

6
When You Can't
Stay the Same

Esther's Story

Based on Esther 4

𝓢*houlders back. Chin high. Hands still.*

Esther's slippered feet beat a rhythmic path back and forth across the polished floor of her sitting room. Her hands ache with the urge to fidget, to sneak a fingernail into a corner of her mouth.

A soft knock taps at the door and Esther's maid, Anna, heaves it open. Esther's fingers hold one another prisoner in front of her waist.

Hathak the eunuch bows in the entryway, his boyish body dwarfed by its massive carved frame. In his delicate hands he twists a scroll. Anna waves him in and then slips back into her corner chair, blending into the furniture, a listening shadow.

"What news from Mordecai?" Esther asks, hoping he doesn't hear the tremor of panic in her voice.

Hathak's brown eyes, usually warm and cheerful, are guarded, uncertain. They keep dropping to his sandals.

"Hathak," Esther says, ducking her head so her face lands in his line of sight. She offers him the platonic version of her most winning smile, the smile she practiced for months to perfect—the smile that exudes kindness and invites openness. This same smile—well, this same smile spiced with a hint of coy playfulness—had induced Xerxes to unburden his royal soul on their very first night together, regaling Esther for hours with tales from his recent battles. "Hathak, you can deliver my cousin's message. It is all right.

I will be all right. Now. . .word for word, if you please."

Hathak blows a long breath out of the corner of his mouth. Esther exhales too. *Shoulders back. Chin high. Hands still.* She threads her skirts through her fingers.

Hathak fixes his gaze on a spot up and to the left of Esther's head, as if he can read Mordecai's words there. "My dear daughter, Hadassah, our people are condemned," Hathak says in his lilting, high-pitched voice. "By order of the king. Plotted and orchestrated by Haman."

"Ha–Haman?" Esther stutters, confused. "Our people?"

"Your people," Hathak says, dropping his voice. "The Jews." His eyes as they meet hers are unreadable.

Esther's stomach gives a sickening roll. She glances back to see if Anna is listening. The stiff angle of her neck says she is. *"In the palace, someone is always listening"*—Hegai's voice, Hegai's warning, Hegai's wisdom.

Not even Hegai knows of Esther's Jewish heritage. Not Hegai, not Anna—not till just now—and certainly not the king. Just as Mordecai had ordered from the beginning, Esther has kept her background secret, but now Mordecai himself has exposed their truth to these servants.

Hathak holds out the scroll in his hands—palms up, two-handed and careful, like an offering. "Mordecai sent this. It's a copy of the edict."

Esther pulls the knotted string free, then begins to read. *On the thirteenth day of the twelfth month, all Jews—young and old, women and children—will be annihilated.* The twisting sensation in her stomach takes on a heavy weight, dragging her under. The scroll falls from her hand. She sags into the couch.

With effort, Esther looks up at Hathak. His face doubles—she stares hard until his two heads blend back into one. "What can be done?" she whispers.

Hathak maintains his distance but kneels. "My lady, Mordecai insists that you must intervene."

"He *what?*" Esther bolts to her feet.

Anna springs forward, a hand supporting Esther's back. "My lady, please lie down," she clucks, a worried hen.

Esther waves her off and gapes at Hathak. "But—but surely my cousin knows I am powerless." She glances at Anna, who gives a rapid series of nods as if to confirm, *Yes, you are powerless. You may be queen, but you are nobody.* "I hold no true influence. I cannot even see the king without a summons."

Esther sits back down, staring at the floor for long, silent moments, her heart thudding limp and anxious in her chest. Not once has she disagreed with Mordecai. Not once resisted. Not once defied. Until now, she has been the picture of submission, everything an obedient daughter—even an adopted one—should be. But this instruction she cannot obey. Surely Mordecai must see. Surely he would not wish her dead.

Esther stands tall, fear granting sudden steadiness. "You must go back to Mordecai and deliver a message."

Hathak rises. His face takes on the fierce look he gets when memorizing.

As Esther begins, she is shocked to find herself fighting—and failing—to keep a touch of resentment, even sarcasm, out of her voice: "All the king's officials—indeed, *all the people of the royal provinces*—know that anyone who approaches the king without a summons will be put to death." She gives Hathak a significant, hard look. He nods; she feels a pulse of vindication. *See, Mordecai? Even the messenger knows you are asking the impossible.* "The only exception is if the king extends the gold scepter and spares his life. But thirty days have passed since I was called to go to the king."

Hathak bows, one eyebrow slightly raised. Esther pivots on her heel, marching to the window. As the door clicks shut behind her, a sandstorm of feelings swirls inside: terror, heartbreak, and—perhaps most upsetting of all—anger. Anger at Mordecai.

Shrugging off Anna's attempts to lead her back to the couch—to make her eat, drink, sit, *submit*—Esther tamps down any lingering shakiness and uses the regal, commanding voice she has practiced in her head but never employed out loud: "I do not require assistance, Anna. I'd like to be alone now. You may wait outside."

Hurt flickers across Anna's lovely features, quickly replaced by a mask of subservience—a mask Esther herself has worn all too many times. "As you wish," Anna whispers, hurrying through the maids' side door. As the door shuts, Esther hears a rustling on the other side, knowing Anna has settled herself against it like a door-stop. Trapping Esther inside, a caged animal. The wealthiest and most privileged of animals, the palace her prison.

Never alone, never free.

White heat flashes across her vision. She is pacing again, making fists again. Her thoughts wage war, one against the other. *Women and children. My people. Mordecai is not wrong to ask. Of course he must ask. But he sends me to certain death! But. . .if not I, then who will save them? . . . And if I fail, who will save me?*

Shadows gather in the corners of the room as sunset bleeds across the sky, but Esther does not summon Anna to light the lamps. As day dies around her, she sits on the couch, still at last.

A knock sounds at the outer door. The maids' door bursts open before Esther even has time to summon help. With a quick, disturbed look around the darkened room, Anna hurries to open the outer door. Hathak stands shadowed and small in the entryway. Esther waves him inside impatiently.

"Well?" she asks.

Behind her, lamps flicker to life, bringing a sallow gloom into the room, casting long, twisting shadows against the walls.

"I have a message from Mordecai, my lady," Hathak says in his soft, boyish voice. "But I—" Shaking his head, he drops his eyes.

Esther steps forward. "Speak freely, Hathak. I do not hold you responsible for the words you carry."

Hathak nods. Blowing air out through the side of his mouth, he fixes his gaze up to the left and begins to recite. His voice starts out soft. "Do not think—" He clears his throat and begins again, stronger this time; his pronunciation hints at Mordecai's accent, the thick breathiness he gives the consonants. "Do not think, dear daughter, that because you are in the king's house you alone of all the Jews will escape." Esther's body goes rigid, her breath thickening to a block in her chest, even as Hathak's voice grows louder, deeper. He mimics Mordecai's cadence, his confident authority: "For if you remain silent at this time, relief and deliverance for the Jews will arise from another place"—as if transported, as if channeling Mordecai's very spirit, Hathak suddenly makes eye contact with Esther—"but *you and your father's family will perish.*" Esther freezes under Hathak's burning gaze, feeling as if Mordecai himself stands before her—he the father figure, she the recalcitrant child. "And who knows but that you have come to royal position for such a time as this?"

For such a time as this.

The words ring in her head. Beat against her heart.

Her own tear-choked voice echoes in her memory:

"But Mordecai, I don't want to go to the palace. I want to stay here with you. Here at home. Why can't I stay with you? Why, why, why?"

Mordecai draws her in close, folding her into his strong arms, where she has always fit—the only fatherly arms she can remember. She ducks her head into the space between his chin and chest, breathes his spicy scent, and unleashes ragged tears. Hours they sit this way—days, years, a girlhood, a lifetime—but Mordecai does not pull back. He strokes her hair just the way she imagines her mother would have done, letting her weep her goodbye and mourn the loss of their life together, and so much more—the loss of the Jewish marriage and family she will never have, because the trip through the palace doors will be a one-way journey. And after a time, he adds his own tears, his broad, solid chest shaking even as it absorbs Esther's sorrow.

"Good will come in the end," he whispers into her hair, choking out the words. "I have to believe that. You must be strong, my girl. Stronger than you think you can be."

Stronger than you think you can be.

For such a time as this.

Esther blinks back to her sitting room with its polished floors. Back to Hathak standing before her, watching her with careful eyes that pretend to see nothing but capture everything. Back to Anna, hovering near in case Esther has another dizzy spell—hovering, protecting, cocooning, like everyone who has ever loved her has always done: first Mordecai, then Hegai, now Hathak and Anna. But none of them can protect her this time.

Esther takes a shaky breath. *Shoulders back. Chin high. Hands still.*

Stronger than you think you can be, my girl.

Only she's not Mordecai's girl anymore—she's not anyone's girl.

She is the queen.

And her time has come.

☙

Pain builds, a small wave swiftly swelling to a tsunami. *This is it,* she thinks, *the most I can hurt without dying.* And then she hurts more. The room fades, her vision bleeds white.

And then the pain ebbs, the vise around her middle relaxing its grip, letting her breathe again, see again. As vision returns, she looks around to find her husband pacing the room—he flashes a way-too-cheerful thumbs-up—and a nurse in a corner humming as she makes notes on a chart. The nurse looks up with a perky grin and chirps, "So how is our pain?" She points to a poster of yellow frowny faces cartooning various stages of misery.

Our pain? OUR pain? Last time I checked, I was the only person in this room in any pain!

And with that thought, something snaps inside. She launches herself off the birthing bed. With a yelp of surprise, her husband leaps to his feet, arms out as if to catch her. She starts yanking sensors and cords off her stomach, chest, and arms, throwing them onto the floor. When the last one falls, she lets out a triumphant, "Ha!"

Her husband stands gaping, mouth working like a fish out of water. She brushes past him, stuffing her legs into sweatpants, one swollen ankle at a time.

"I don't want to do this anymore. I'm"—she pants, breathing through a contraction—"I'm—going—home."

"You're *what*?" her husband and the nurse say in chorus.

She waddles for the door in her sweatpants, hospital gown, and fuzzy blue socks. Her voice is shrill. "I'm a doctor! I know what I'm doing!" As she lumbers through the doorframe, skidding a little on the shiny linoleum, several nurses round the corner from the nurses' station. "Dr. Smith, please stop," says the posse's front-runner, in the kind of overly patient voice you use with a two-year-old throwing a tantrum. Or a psycho waving a gun.

"No!" Dr. Smith shouts, huffing toward the exit door. "I am not having a baby today!"

∽

This is my attempt at recreating a story my mom told me about the way her friend—a physician!—responded when labor got hard. "Dr. Smith" had been taking care of her own patients for years, had read all the books and thoroughly understood—in theory—what to expect, but when labor pains arrived, she tried to run away. Where she thought she was going and how she thought she was going to reverse the unstoppable process God had initiated in her womb, I do not know. (I don't think she knew either.)

Have you ever been Dr. Smith? Stuck in a situation so painful, so scary, so overwhelming, that you just can't deal? You just want *out*? All you can think is *run*?

Esther has already suffered—already overcome—so much. Taken from her home, her family, her friends. Forced to abandon whatever hopes and plans she'd had for her life. Taken into the palace, never to return. And against all odds, Esther has risen to be queen. Hasn't she suffered enough? Doesn't she deserve to just sit around enjoying the benefits of her glamorous prison?

Have you ever felt that way? Like you've already put in your time, already given enough and lost too much? Like no one (not even God) is allowed to ask any more of you? I bet Esther felt that way.

I bet Moses felt that way. And Jeremiah. And Peter. And pretty much everyone else in the Bible whom God called to go.

But no. God needs more from Esther. Here in this fraught moment, Esther has a choice to make: Run from danger, pretend it doesn't exist, hide in the palace while her people are slaughtered. Or confront the peril: face her fears, face her husband, face herself—and let God decide the outcome.

In this moment, Esther can't stay the same.

A New Kind of Courage

Until now, Esther has survived by obeying. By keeping quiet, following instructions, hiding in plain sight. She has survived under the care and protection of a series of men (Mordecai, Hegai, Hathak) who have guarded her and guided her.

And now Mordecai is asking her to turn all her survival skills on their head: speak up, act fast. . .and stand alone. There will be no one whispering advice and encouragement as she bows trembling before the king. No one to speak for her, no one to defend her. No one to step between Esther and the sword if things go sideways. Esther has to stand alone. She has to be brave. Brav*er*. A whole new level of brave.

Because let's give Esther the credit she deserves: She is no wimp. It has already taken great courage to leave home and build a life in the palace, to win the hand—and heart—of a king. These are no small feats, and hers is no small courage. But this is going to take a whole new level of courage.

Esther can't stay the same.

When There's No Way Out

I am sitting on my bed in a tangle of blankets, a puddle of tears. It's been a hard year—so much loss, such a short time. A year earlier, in a dizzying three-week span, we had lost a pregnancy—a loved and celebrated pregnancy—at the same time that we unexpectedly moved two states away from family and friends to start a new church alongside strangers in a new town.

We had stumbled into town hurting, lonely, and a little lost (*literally* lost—I kept getting turned around in my own labyrinthine neighborhood). We were excited about building a new church, but some days, it was hard to be inspired. Hard to see past the crushing needs of *today*. Hard to think beyond the sometimes overwhelming needs of three delightful miracle kids who were the joy of our lives but who *never stopped needing*. Hard to think about saving souls when I just wanted a good night's sleep. Hard to see past the endless laundry, the dishes that never stopped piling, the bills that wouldn't let us catch our breath.

I had gotten pregnant again—praise God in His goodness—and life seemed a bit more hopeful. And then, our first summer in our new hometown, we decided to escape the lonely and drive a gazillion miles to visit my parents in their new South Florida home. We packed three kids and enough Goldfish and gummy bears to survive a hard winter on the Oregon Trail, and set off down I-95. As we hit the beautiful city of Jacksonville, Florida, our old-but-paid-for minivan started bumping and rattling. Let's pick up the story there. . . .

Kevin casts me a nervous fake smile. "It's probably fine," he says. "I mean, I'm totally sure it's fine. I'm just going to have someone check it out before we set off on the final leg."

"I see," I say, sniffing out one of Kevin's "If I tell Elizabeth nothing is wrong, then she'll think nothing is wrong even though it definitely is" tricks. "You're totally sure, but. . .the mechanic will help you be *sure* you are totally sure?"

"Exactly."

So we check into our hotel. I take the kids to the pool; Kevin takes the car to the shop. After a while Kevin calls me. "So the van is dead," he says.

"What do you mean, *dead*? You don't mean. . .dead?"

"Is there another kind?"

I sniff into the phone.

"So. . . ," Kevin says, "I am buying us a new van. Well, a new old van."

"But–but–but we don't have any money. We need the paid-for van to last another two years."

"D-e-a-d."

"Don't they have, like, car defibrillators?"

"Dead as a doornail."

"Can't Jesus resurrect it if we pray really, really hard?"

"The mechanic said it might explode. Do you want to make our children explode on I-95?"

I grunt into the phone, swallowing the urge to be snarky and quip, *"I have my moments."*

We hang up and Pregnant and Extremely Hormonal-Slash-Emotional Elizabeth calls her dad. He picks up the phone and P&EHSE Elizabeth starts sobbing. "It's official. I'm a Barefoot, Pregnant Preacher's Wife. We're living off of discount peanut butter and jelly bought with coupons, and now our van might explode and we can't pay our bills already and now we're going to have a car payment and we're going to the poorhouse and did I mention I'm barefoot—*literally barefoot because I'm at the pool*—and pregnant and my minivan might explode?"

My poor father tries to say some comforting things.

But I have hit a breaking point. Flash-forward a few months and I am sitting on our bed in the tangle of sheets, the puddle of tears, telling Kevin, "I can't. I can't do this. I can't be away from family and friends and starting a new church in a strange city and so daggum stressed about money all the daggum time. I can't do this anymore. I need something to change. I need a break. I. Can't. Do. This."

My poor husband sits silent, and through the haze of tears I can see my words gutting him.

But many hours later, when I finally start praying, I (grudgingly) come to this: I may feel like I can't do this—our life—but. . .*I have to do it*. I have no other choice. There is nothing to do except get up again the next day, keep working, keep paying down debt, keep making PB&Js bought on sale with coupons, keep making the daggum minivan payment, keep missing home, keep making new friends, keep on keeping on.

Saying "I can't" did nothing but make me feel powerless and my husband feel terrible. The only way *out* was *through*. Through the long days, the hard months, the lonely years.

Just like for Esther, when the only way out of her people's danger was through the king's doorway; just like for Dr. Smith that day in the labor and delivery room, when the only way out of pregnancy was for that baby to come through the birth canal—the only way out of my problems was to go through them. To *grow* through them.

Sometimes problems arise and we manage to find a way around them. We just change direction and—*woo-hoo!*—we've sidestepped the crisis. When that happens, yay for us. But sometimes God has us in circumstances we can't escape. No way around, no way out. Sometimes He puts us in, or allows us to remain in, situations that expose our every doubt, fear, and weakness. They range from the inconvenient to the catastrophic: A class you can't drop. A conflict you can't avoid. A financial disaster. A family drama. A sick child. An unexpected death.

We cannot run from these situations. Some are griefs that feel past bearing, past surviving—and yet we must bear them. We must survive them. The only way out is through. And in situations like this, God is saying, "Grow." He gives us no choice but to move forward. No choice but to change.

Maybe we have to become stronger. More resilient. Willing to take on a challenge we'd rather avoid. Or maybe we have to become "weaker." More vulnerable. Willing to accept—even invite—help. Maybe, like Esther, we have to become braver. More independent. Willing to stand alone. Whatever our demons, we have to take them on and wrestle them down till we sit on top, bloodied but victorious.

We *Get* to Change

One of my favorite things about being a Christian is that *we get to change*. Most people you know are probably still the same basic people they've always been since late adolescence—just taller and less pimply. But their character, their strengths and weaknesses—those have stayed mostly the same. Christians are no better than anyone else, but thanks to the grace of God, the blood of Christ, and the power of the Spirit, you and I get to grow and change. What a wondrous, liberating gift! You know all those flaws you hate about yourself? Those weaknesses that frustrate you, embarrass you, and limit you? With God's help we can change them! We can grow. *We can grow*, and what a privilege that is! Paul paints us vivid pictures of spiritual growth in his letters:

> *Yet, my brothers, I do not consider myself to have "arrived" spiritually, nor do I consider myself already perfect. But I keep going on, grasping ever more firmly that purpose for which Christ grasped me. My brothers, I do not consider myself to have fully grasped it even now. But I do concentrate on this: I leave the past behind and with hands outstretched to whatever lies ahead I go straight for the goal—my reward the honour of being called by God in Christ.*
> PHILIPPIANS 3:12–14 PHILLIPS

When There's No Other Way

My friend calls, and I can hear the tremor in her voice, the tears threatening. I suspect it's only shock keeping them in check. "He did it again," she whispers. "You know, the addiction stuff. He's willing to get help, he wants to change—truly, he does—but. . .I don't know how we'll get through this. And the kids. . ."

My heart crashes.

There is not much to say. I tell her I'm sorry; I promise to pray. And pray I do.

We've shared a lot of life together, this friend and I. Like me, she has *so many feelings*. It's why I adore her, why we are friends. You know that saying, "What doesn't kill you makes you stronger"? With us it has always been more like, "What doesn't kill you leaves you twitching and gasping in the ditch for a very long time." And so I wonder how in the world she will find the strength to survive this.

Because if she's going to survive—and she *has* to survive—then she has no choice but to keep going forward. If she wants her marriage and family to stay together—and she does; in spite of the pain, in spite of it all, she does—then she has to grow stronger than she has ever been. The only way out is through.

I step back and watch my friend fight.

I watch her show her husband tough love—very tough love—without running from him and his demons.

I watch her swallow tears when her children are watching, to protect them.

I watch her keep going to work.

I watch her keep going to church, keep giving to others.

Most of all, I watch her keep going to God. Begging Him for strength, wisdom, and help she cannot give her husband or herself. God gives them all, and I stand amazed. Like Esther, my friend becomes someone she never knew she could be, because she has no other choice. She can't stay the same. She can't collapse in a puddle of tears the way we used to. She can't wallow. Can't hide.

Can't throw a pity party and ask me to bring the decorations. She has to rise *to* this, rise *above* this. And so she rises.

It Starts in Your Head

When the only way out is through, when you can't stay the same, the first battle is the one we fight with ourselves. The one with our thoughts and attitudes about the situation. Like Esther, when we get the call to *go*, we have to respond. And at first, Esther's message back to Mordecai is, to paraphrase, "Are you insane? I can't do that!"

Can we talk about those two crippling words: *I can't*?

Because I have said those words too many times in my life:

"I can't do this."

"I can't deal with this."

"I can't keep living in (whatever situation I don't want to be in)."

"I can't do (that thing God wants me to do)."

Can't.

The thing is, with God on our side, very few things are actually *can't*-level things.

And can we be honest about what we're really saying when we say, "I can't"? When we say, "I can't," most of the time we're really saying, "I won't."

When I sat there throwing a pregnant pity party on my bed, first of all. . .I was hormonal and tired, and honestly, I couldn't help being hormonal and tired. I was more than just physically tired; I was deep-down-in-my-soul tired. I was *weary*. And it was okay to be weary. To feel sad. To confess frustration and confusion. To seek help and communicate need. All that would have been fine. But the problem came in when I said, "I can't." That's where the conversation turned. Because with those words and that attitude, I put myself—and God—in a box. Not just a box, a prison. A prison of my own design.

"For I can do everything through Christ, who gives me strength," wrote Paul (Philippians 4:13 NLT). "All things are possible with God," promised Jesus (Mark 10:27).

When we say, "I can't," we write off God's power, His promises. And what is the alternative anyway? To crawl into bed and hide under the covers until we die? What was the alternative for Esther? To hide behind her crown and watch her people be massacred?

Maybe the old Esther couldn't do this.

Maybe yesterday's Esther couldn't do this.

But today's Esther had no choice.

Kevin and I recently took our eight-year-old, Avery, out to learn how to ride a bike. When we got her settled on her bike, she blinked up at us from beneath her huge helmet, crocodile tears threatening. "I can't ride a bike!" she insisted. Now here's the thing you should know about Avery: she is one of the most naturally gifted athletes I have ever met. There is no doorframe she cannot climb, no balance beam she cannot conquer—but a bike without training wheels. . .well, that was new.

As I stood there wringing my hands (classic Mom), Kevin insisted (classic Dad), "Sure you can! Let's go!" And without giving Avery time to work up to full-blown Panic Mode (I maintain she did *not* inherit Panic Mode from me), he grabbed her bike seat and started pushing her down the street, jogging alongside. Avery had no choice but to pedal, but the whole time she was shrieking, "I can't, I can't, I can't!" After a few yards Kevin let go. . .and Avery kept speeding down the street, hollering, "I can't, I can't, I can't!"— *even as she proved herself wrong.*

Isn't that what we do with God so many times? He assures us we are ready for a challenge and pushes us out of our comfort zone. We zoom along, pedaling furiously, fighting and crying and screaming, "I can't do this!"—but the fact is, *we are already doing it.* The fact is, with God we can.

During a time of intense persecution and suffering, the apostle Paul wrote:

But we have this treasure in jars of clay to show

*that this all-surpassing power is from God and not
from us. We are hard pressed on every side, but not
crushed; perplexed, but not in despair; persecuted, but
not abandoned; struck down, but not destroyed. We
always carry around in our body the death of Jesus, so
that the life of Jesus may also be revealed in our body.
For we who are alive are always being given over
to death for Jesus' sake, so that his life may also be
revealed in our mortal body.*

2 Corinthians 4:7–11

Do you hear that?

Paul and his companions were hard pressed, *but not crushed.*

They were perplexed—confused, unsure why God was allowing them to suffer—*but not in despair.*

They were persecuted, *but not abandoned.*

They had been struck down, *but not destroyed.*

The next time you are tempted to shut down, to run off, to stop growing; the next time you are tempted to shout, "But Lord, I can't," remember this: Maybe *you* can't. . .but God can. And maybe, with God, you already are.

When It's Time to Tackle *That Weakness*

Several months into our marriage, I burst into tears over. . .honestly, I have no idea. Probably something to do with feeling overwhelmed in our schedule, or feeling guilty about something, or maybe just the price of cereal. Kevin looked at me with a funny glint in his eye and teased, "I never knew I had married a sprinkler."

Ha-ha-ha-*ha.* (Please read that line with a heavy dose of sarcasm.)

Poor Kevin didn't fully understand what an emotional roller coaster he had signed up for when he married me, but he soon found out. With me, there are a lot of feelings. And by a lot, I mean a *lot.* And by a *lot* I mean more than one poor husband (or one poor me, for that matter) should have to manage.

At first, he found the feelings cute. The crying was kind of cute too—it made my eyes turn green. But after a while, it got a little. . .well, it got to be a little *a lot*.

When I was in high school and college, I used to fall into these things my family affectionately called "funks." I would get down about something—usually I was feeling guilty or anxious about something dumb—and then I would just shut down. Disappear into my head and my dark thoughts. Wander around quiet and brooding. It might take me days to pull out. Looking back, I realize my "funks" weren't so much depression as prolonged pouting. (As those of you who have experienced legitimate depression can attest, there is an important difference involving brain chemicals and lots of fancy terminology I won't attempt to define here.)

I have a dog named Cole. The moment you start scratching his ears, Cole immediately flops over onto his back as if to say, "Rub my belly. I'm at your mercy." That was me with my funks. I didn't really try to resist—sadness would come scratching at my ear and I would immediately flop down on the floor, belly up. The funks weren't that big of a deal when I had my own room and I could shut the door and brood in private.

But then I indulged in a couple of funks as a young married woman. Poor Kevin. Kevin is a happy guy. He whistles around the house for absolutely no reason except random happiness: the smell of cut grass, the thought of ice cream, the existence of football. He thanks God at the end of every single day, no matter how boring or depressing or blah that day was, for a "wonderful day"—and he means it with all of his happy little heart, *every single time*. (I find this kind of relentless optimism baffling. But also adorable.)

So poor happy Kevin didn't know what to do with his new funky wife. He kept trying to fix me, but of course the whole point was that I didn't feel like being fixed. I had decided, "I can't. I can't get over things quickly. I can't *not* brood. This is just the way I am, and I like me this way."

But I started to notice a difference in my new husband. Bless him, if I wasn't happy, he wasn't happy. He felt like me not being happy in general was me not being happy with him. And I realized with a rather unpleasant jolt that it was time for me to grow emotionally. Maybe I had been this way for a long time, maybe I had gotten away with it when the only person deeply affected by my own feelings was me. . .but I was married now. I had promised to love, honor, and protect. And I was hurting my husband by refusing even to *try* to change. So I started working on myself.

I started fighting back against the funk instead of just immediately going belly-up, Cole-style. I started opening up more to people and letting them help me work through my tangled thoughts and feelings. I started building up an arsenal of scriptures to help me fight wayward thoughts: "Overcome evil with good" (Romans 12:21), "Rejoice in the Lord always" (Philippians 4:4), "Cast all your anxiety on him because he cares for you" (1 Peter 5:7), "Take captive every thought" (2 Corinthians 10:5).

When I was tempted to "go there"—to cross the line from "Hmm, I had kind of a rough day" to "I'm going to wallow in this and just lie here like wilted spinach for a few days"—I fought back. I made imperfect progress, but I made steps forward. Kevin's whistling started up again. It's been eighteen years. I'm still growing, but Kevin's still whistling.

This is my story—what's yours? Because can we just say that *feelings* are a difficult issue for a lot of us? Feelings are beautiful, a wondrous gift from God—the ability to be happy so hard it hurts, to laugh, to rant, to mourn, to love. But as with all of God's gifts, Satan wants to flip those blessings around and warp them for his purposes.

To turn our capacity for love into selfish obsession.

To turn our admiration of beautiful things into greed.

To turn innocent friendship into inappropriate attraction.

To turn godly sorrow into crippling regret.

To turn our desire for peace into addictive behavior.

To turn healthy grief into destructive depression.

Feelings are complicated, but God's wise guidelines in the scriptures can help give our emotions healthy, godly boundaries. They can help us learn to say, "You can go here. . .and no further."[1]

When Our "I Can't" Hurts Others

Esther's story reveals a powerful impetus for change: other people. We don't live in a vacuum. Our words, our choices, and even our feelings can affect people around us. Sometimes we get stuck in a rut, refusing to grow or change. But what if we realize our stubbornness or complacency or fear may be harming another person? That's what happened to me with Kevin. That's what happened to Esther with the Jews. She couldn't pretend that her inaction would have no consequences. She wasn't convinced to change based on principle alone, or even on the desire to please God; no, Esther chose to change to save people.

Is there something you have refused to change—or been afraid to change—until now? Some pet sin, some limiting weakness? Take a look around at the people you love and ask yourself if your inaction is affecting others.

Maybe you have been stuck in an addiction for a long time, and you won't change for yourself, but you are beginning to see the harm it is doing to people you love: parents, friends, spouse, children.

Maybe you have always had a temper, and you have always told yourself, "This is just the way I am. I blow my top sometimes, but everyone knows this about me and I make it up to them"—but now God has put a sensitive person in your life who is being wounded by your outbursts, and you realize you can't rationalize the behavior anymore.

My friend Emma is one of the most brilliant and lovable people ever to grace this planet, but as every superhero must have a built-in vulnerability (because otherwise their perfection would be unbearable), so Emma has hers, and it's airplanes. Airplanes are her kryptonite. A terrifying experience with turbulence many years ago left her traumatized. Having watched my own husband battle a near-crippling fear of flying, I have great respect for this type of claustrophobia. It's a real thing—primal, unwanted, overpowering. For fifteen years, Emma managed to avoid air travel.

But then her beloved stepdaughter decided to get married. . .in Jamaica. Emma had three choices: hurt Katlin by refusing to attend the wedding, sell the house so she could hire a private yacht and crew to sail her to Jamaica, or. . .get on an airplane and fly to Jamaica.

When Emma first called me to tell me she had to fly, she was choking back tears. I nearly cried with her, knowing how visceral a fear this was, knowing how her sleep would be haunted for all the long months leading up to the flight. We took to speaking in code, calling it D-Day (for me this meant "Determination Day"; for Emma I suspect it meant "Death Day"). As D-Day approached, Emma got sick, as if her body itself was resisting her decision. But Emma was determined to get on that plane. We prayed together, and I, helpful friend that I am, attempted to suggest entertaining strategies for flight survival, everything from in-flight intravenous infusions of sleeping medicine, to laughing gas, to frying pans to the face. (Emma was not amused.) When she got on that plane, I started praying. While Emma battled her fears on the plane, I waged war on the ground.

John writes, "Perfect love drives out fear" (1 John 4:18). And while I doubt John had claustrophobia and airplane anxiety in mind when he penned that scripture, it holds a universal truth: we conquer fear when we love. Emma got on that plane because she loves Katlin more than she loves herself. Emma got on that plane because she loves Katlin more than she fears her fear.

In the end, my friends, *love* is why we change. When we want to stay the same, love forces our hand. When it's easier to hide in a hole, to stay safe on the ground, we change because we love. So if it's time for you to change—if God is forcing your hand and you can't stay the same—know this: God is love and love gives strength. Love conquers fear.

One Step at a Time

It is comforting to realize that Esther didn't go straight to the king and blurt out the whole situation as soon as she received Mordecai's message. No, she took things one step at a time.

First she fasted and prayed. She took her problem to God. (So far, so good!)

Then she went and stood in the doorway of the king's antechamber. King Xerxes extended his scepter, inviting Esther to enter his presence. (So far, so good!)

Then she walked through the doorway, across the room, up to the king, and requested a banquet. He said yes. (So far, so good!)

Day by day, hurdle by hurdle, step by step, Esther kept moving forward until she saved her people. You and I must do the same. We must keep moving forward. We need not jump ahead ten steps, or even ten days—let's just move forward one step at a time.

Let's allow God to make us braver than we think we can be. Let's quiet the voice that insists, "I can't." Like the Little Engine That Could, with every step let's whisper, "I think I can. . ." because even when *we* can't, our God can.

Let's Go Deeper. . .

For Further Study

You can read Esther's full story in the short book of Esther.

Journal Prompt

1. Fill in the blank: "I can't _____." What will it take for you to say, "But God can"?

2. Has God ever proven you wrong when you told Him, "I can't _____"? How?

3. Can you identify a weakness in your life that can't stay the same? What first step would help you to begin changing it?

Prayer Prompt

For those who are led by the Spirit of God are the children of God. The Spirit you received does not make you slaves, so that you live in fear again; rather, the Spirit you received brought about your adoption to sonship. And by him we cry, "Abba, Father." The Spirit himself testifies with our spirit that we are God's children. Now if we are children, then we are heirs—heirs of God and co-heirs with Christ, if indeed we share in his sufferings in order that we may also share in his glory. I consider that our present sufferings are not worth comparing with the glory that will be revealed in us.
Romans 8:14–18

7
When You Used to Be Brave

The Story of Mary the Mother of Jesus, Part 2

Based on Luke 4:14–30 and Mark 3:20–35

The mob swallows her screams. No one hears. No one turns. No one cares.

Their words are swords. "Liar!" "Blasphemer!" "Son of Satan!"

She can still see her son, but barely—through the writhing tangle of red faces, angry elbows, flying fists, she catches flashes of blue, the blue robe she made for Him.

"No! Stop!" she screams, the words shredding her throat. She's lost her mind; she's lost her place. She flies into the crowd, feet kicking, arms flailing. A stray elbow knocks her in the face and she sprawls into dirt, dizzied and bleeding.

One fierce voice pierces the noise: "Death to the heretic!"

The mob picks up the cry, turns it into a chant: "Death! Death! Death!"

The crowd surges forward in a cloud of dust, a tumble of hate. A blue-clad arm breaks through the bodies, grasping at air—a familiar hand, a hand she has held a thousand times, reaching for help, reaching for her—and disappears. The mob rushes toward the cliff to throw Him over the edge, to break His body, bury it beneath stones.

"Jesus!" she screams.

She wakes, shrieking, to darkness. Hot tears in her mouth, cold fear in her chest. Her bed a soaked and tangled mess of nightmares. Her hand reaches through the sheets, through the dark, to find Joseph, to find comfort in his arms.

Reality returns—fresh pain, a burning lance. *Not there. Long dead.* She sits up, teeth chattering, lungs heaving. She breathes slow, seeks calm. *Just a dream, just a dream.*

But it's not just a dream. Jesus escaped the mob once in Nazareth; next time he may not be so lucky. Mary has to bring Him home, show Him there are better ways to serve God—quieter ways, wiser ways, *safer* ways.

Still shaking, she crawls out of bed, lights a candle, and hurries to the curtained entrance to the tiny room James shares with his wife. "James!" she whispers. Inside she hears a muffled groan. Seconds later, the curtain twitches and her son's face appears. "Mother? Are you all right?" His eyes, puffy with sleep, squint in the soft light.

She pulls her shoulders back. "I need you to gather your brothers."

James rubs his face with his hands—hands like Joseph's: long fingers, thick knuckles, woodworking scars. He mutters muffled words into his palms.

"*What* did you say?" Mary puts thunder in the words.

James places his hands on her shoulders. Mischief twinkles past the tiredness in his eyes. "I *said*, my beloved, beautiful mother, your wish is my command, but. . . it's the middle of the night."

Mary narrows her eyes and shrugs out of his hands. "Did your father and I complain when an angel woke us in the middle of the night and told us to flee to Egypt to save your brother's life?"

James holds up both palms, mingling a laugh with a sigh. "I'm not sure this is the same situation—unless. . ." He raises one eyebrow. "You haven't had another angelic visitor, have you?"

"No." She tosses her braid over one shoulder. "Not exactly. But I had a—a dream—and we're going to get Jesus. We're going to bring Him home."

"A *dream*?" He pries the candle from her still-shaking hands and places it on a small table. "Mother—"

Mary pokes a finger into his chest. Thumps his heart with each word. "*He's going to get Himself killed*. You have to help me stop Him." She drops her finger, makes fists at her sides. "Please."

"Mother, I'm sorry, but is it possible you're. . .overreacting?" He winces even as the last word leaves his lips.

"*Overreacting?*" She grinds the word out through clenched teeth.

James tries a wheedling smile and pinches air between his thumb and finger. "Just a little bit?"

"James, I am *under*reacting!" she says, her voice hitting a dangerous pitch. James throws a nervous look back over his shoulder. "Mother, you'll wake the house."

She drops her voice to an angry hiss. "*You* try wrangling a family without a husband. *You* try reining in a son who keeps kicking the anthill, provoking the Pharisees." Her throat tastes of tears. "Have I not given enough? Have I not lost enough? I can't lose Jesus too. I can't."

James gives one of his quiet nods and folds her into an embrace. For a moment she sags into him, wetting his tunic with tears. His shape, his scent, are so much like Joseph's, she is dizzied by memory.

"He's taking this whole save-the-world thing too far," she says into his chest. "Just like that time at the temple when He was a boy. He gets carried away, lost in the moment. But now. . .now I'm worried He's lost His mind."

"This is new information?" James's teasing laughter rumbles into the side of her head.

She tips her head back to meet his eyes. "This is serious, James."

His eyes soften in a smile. "I know. But Mother. . ." He inhales and puts on his gentle voice, his Joseph voice. "Are you sure we should stop Him? What if—what if this is what He's supposed to do?"

"After everything God put us through to get Him here?" she chokes out, pushing James away. "No. *No*. He is a gift—*my* gift, straight from heaven. Jesus is meant to save us all, and He can't do that if He's dead. This—all this conflict, all this danger—this is not the plan." She lets the words hang, repeating them in her mind till she almost believes them.

James's gentle voice pushes on. "But what if He knows exactly what He's doing, and we just. . .we just have to be brave enough to support Him?"

"Brave enough? *Brave enough?*" Mary steps back and glares up at James, fury making her jaw tremble. "Don't you talk to me about brave, James son of Joseph!"

James holds up his palms—surrender—and steps forward, wrapping her fists in his warm hands. "You are the bravest person I know, Mother."

She opens her fists and looks down at her hands, lined now by veins and time. She wilts. "I am an old woman," she whispers, "and I have had enough of being brave."

After a long pause, James tips her chin up and says, "Mother, I don't think we get to choose when we're done being brave."

Mary looks away. At last she crosses her arms and says, "You were supposed to object."

"To which part?"

She smacks him on the arm. "The part about me being old!"

James laughs. "I just—" He shakes his head, swallowing his words. "Of course I'll go with you, Mother. I won't let you lose Him. I'll wake Jude and the rest, and we'll go get Jesus."

"Really?" She smiles, victorious. Pauses for a second, then snaps her fingers. "Why aren't you moving?"

The next day, Mary stands in front of a large house, her sons lined like a wall of protection behind her. "Speaking of kicked anthills," James says, leaping sideways to dodge a group of squealing children, "that's exactly what this house looks like. Only the ants are people."

Clusters of men linger in open doorways, standing on tiptoe to peer inside; teenagers perch in windowsills, legs kicking and dangling; families with small children sit on blankets outside. Every nearby tree provides shade for sick people lying on mats.

"All these people are here to see *Jesus*?" says James.

"Well, either *they* are crazy, or He is," says Jude, and the brothers all laugh.

Mary shoots Jude a look.

James hails a wiry boy kicking rocks. "Think you can get into that house to deliver a message?" James opens his palm to reveal coins.

The boy squints from the coins to the crowd, then grins. "Yes, sir. Easy, sir."

Mary steps forward. "Find Jesus, the one they call Teacher. Tell Him His mother and brothers need to speak with Him. The faster you go, the more we pay."

The boy nods and dives into the crowd, weaving and bobbing. His dark head disappears. A few minutes later he sprints back, chest heaving.

"Well?" says Jude. "Is He coming?"

The boy shakes his head no, biting his lip. His eyes dart from James to Mary to the ground, like birds afraid to land.

"No?" Mary says, louder than she means to. "Why not?"

Placing a calming hand on Mary's shoulder, James asks the boy, "Did He say anything?"

The boy speaks to his sandals. "He said, 'Who are My mother and brothers?'"

Mary gasps.

"He did this"—the boy spreads his arms wide and looks around in a semicircle—"and said, 'Here are My mother and My brothers! Whoever does God's will is My brother and sister and mother.'"

With a soft cry, Mary steps back, hands on her heart. James's arms come around her. He presses a kiss onto the top of her head. "Mother, let's go."

When first we meet Mary, her faith and courage leap off the page. In a single moment, Mary's life changes, and in that same moment, Mary accepts and adapts. No negotiating, no complaining, no "Why me, God?" She simply says, "I am the Lord's servant. May it be to me as you have said."

But fast-forward thirty years to the beginning of Jesus' ministry, to the scene we just explored. Here we find a different Mary—a Mary who, fearing for her son, misunderstanding His role, tries to pull Him out of ministry. To set Him straight and keep Him safe.

For a long time, I didn't get this interaction between Mary and her son. Didn't understand how she got to this place. I thought, *Is this the same Mary? Did she forget everything she knew about her own son? She knew He could do miracles—why then would she call Him crazy? How did she decide she knew better than Jesus and she needed to take over?* (*Ahem.* She is a human. This is our struggle. But it was so much more than that. . . .)

But now, here at the beginning of my forties, a mother of four precious souls—now, living each day in a place of terrifying vulnerability, with four pieces of my heart walking around outside my body—now I think I understand.

You know what I think happened to Mary? I think *life* happened. Mary endured agonies only hinted at in the pages of scripture. First, disgrace and near divorce because of a suspect pregnancy.

Soon after Jesus' birth, Mary faces an unexpected nighttime flight to Egypt to save her son's life. Does she know Herod has already killed dozens of baby boys in his hunt for her son? Does she go through life carrying that awful awareness, that crushing weight? The threat from Herod is Mary's first bitter taste of the knowledge that her son will always have a target on His back. How did Mary adapt to this new life raising a beloved child—a child shining and gifted, with a heart more beautiful than any other on earth (we all think this of our children, but in Mary's case *it was true*)—always in the shadow of death?

Still new to marriage and motherhood, Mary spends two years in a foreign land without the support of family or friends. She returns home to raise a boy she adores but does not fully understand (see Luke 2:41–52). She spends a decade or so having more babies, raising a family.[1] Somewhere along the way—sometime between Jesus' twelfth year and the beginning of His ministry some twenty years later—it seems that she loses her husband.[2]

What all this did to Mary's heart we can only guess. I can imagine what it would have done to mine.

Has *life* happened to you? Joys so staggering you can't put them into words, can't share them with anyone but God? Gifts so precious and rare that their worth consumes you, overwhelms you—makes you vulnerable, your heart no longer your own—and you know if you lose the gift you'll shatter beyond repair?

Has life thrown you detours and delays you never expected? Hurts and betrayals you want to forgive but cannot forget? Disappointments and regrets that haunt your thoughts and steal your contentment? We all live life and we all have scars.

And it was more than just life that happened to Mary; *fear* happened. Fear casts a long shadow, a dark one. Jesus' very first sermon in His own hometown of Nazareth nearly got Him killed—did you realize that? If Mary—alone now, a widow—has ever cherished secret dreams of her son becoming a respected rabbi, how quickly those dreams have turned to nightmares. The Bible mentions the incident so calmly, so briefly, it's easy to read past the drama, the horror, and even—there at the end—the hidden humor. At first, Jesus' sermon is going great:

> *All spoke well of him and were amazed at the*
> *gracious words that came from his lips. "Isn't this*
> *Joseph's son?" they asked.*
>
> LUKE 4:22

But the sermon isn't over. Jesus goes on, challenging their racism, and then the crowd turns:

> *All the people in the synagogue were furious when*
> *they heard this. They got up, drove him out of*
> *the town, and took him to the brow of the hill on*
> *which the town was built, in order to throw him*
> *off the cliff. But he walked right through the crowd*
> *and went on his way.*
>
> LUKE 4:28–30

I wonder if Mary was there that day, first blushing with pride as her boy dazzled His hometown crowd. How quickly pride must have turned to anxiety as Jesus deliberately provoked them, exposing their racism. How quickly anxiety must have turned to terror as the town formed a mob and drove Him—most likely carried Him, kicking and writhing—to a cliff to kill Him. And this was no mob of strangers—these were Mary's neighbors, Jesus' childhood friends, maybe even a few relatives. The whole town is consumed with rage, disaster is at hand, and then—Jesus just walks away. Calms the storm. Parts the crowd. *This isn't My day, people. My time is coming, and soon—but not here, not now.* He gives them a sad smile, a small wave, and walks Himself home. Home to Mary, most likely. They all stand there panting, coming down off the frenzy. Avoiding eye contact. Muttering a few lingering complaints. Eventually the entire town shuffles home. We can only hope they felt shame.

A mother doesn't recover from an ordeal like that. She can never forget. A trauma involving our loved ones does something to us inside. And if we don't *do something* about the something—the terror, the helplessness, the crippling realization that we are not in control, that even though we would die for the people we love we cannot always keep them safe—if we do not surrender those feelings to the hands of Almighty God, the fear takes over.

Fear unbound does ugly things:
Unbound fear binds our hearts.
Unbound fear erodes our trust.
Unbound fear darkens our perception of people.
Unbound fear brings out our controlling nature.
Unbound fear distances us from God.
Mary's fear took over, and so *Mary* tried to take over.

When You Used to Be Brave

I've gone snow skiing twice in my life: the first time when I was a twenty-four-year-old newlywed, the second time when I was a thirty-seven-year-old mother of four. Oh, what a difference thirteen years (and four kids) makes!

The first time, we skied on a short but steep North Carolina slope with horrible snow—aka *a thick sheet of ice*, aka *a death trap for new skiers with no idea how to turn or—more importantly—stop.*

When we went up on the ski lift for the first time, here's what happened:

> Kevin (*Gets off the lift, his back turned to me. Doesn't realize I've clambered off behind him. Turns around to help me, saying*): "So Elizabeth, if you want to turn or slow down, you need to—" *Leaps out of the path of a blue blur that nearly bulldozes him to the ground. The blue blur is shrieking like a banshee. Seconds later Kevin realizes the blue blur is his wife.*
>
> Me (*careening down the icy slope at Olympic speed*): "How do I stoooooooooop?"
>
> Kevin: *Panics, chasing me down the slope, pulling out speed and tricks he hasn't attempted since his teenage years skiing black diamonds in Colorado.*
>
> Me (*to the other skiers I'm barreling past*): "Out of my way! Out of my way! I don't know how to tuuuuuuuuuuurn!"

Kevin: *Weaves around an obstacle course of fallen skiers who have had to dive out of my way. Prays I don't break my neck before he catches me.*

When Kevin finally skids to a stop at the bottom, his frantic eyes comb the fence, seeking the shattered remains of his new wife's broken body. He finds me lying in a blue heap beside the fence. . .and howling with laughter.

Me (*shouting up at him from the snow*): "That was the most amazing thing *ever*! Let's go again!"
Kevin (*helping me up, not sure if he wants to kill me or kiss me*): "First let's have a little lesson on turning and braking."
Me (*already dashing toward the ski lift*): "Okay, you can teach me on the way up."

We tear up and down that icy slope all day. I never learn how to brake, but I have the time of my life, crashing to a stop at the bottom every time. Kevin feels like the luckiest man alive because he has unknowingly married an adrenaline junkie. Oh, the adventures we can have now that he knows this about me! There's nothing his rock-star-slash-gorgeous-athlete-of-a wife won't try! (Okay, he probably wasn't thinking those adjectives. I just added them because this is my book and it's fun to pretend.)

Fast-forward thirteen years. We're now thirty-seven, and in honor of our fifteenth anniversary, we're taking an Epic Ski Trip to Whistler, BC, Canada. I have not skied one time since that glorious day when I was twenty-four. I'm a little nervous, but mostly excited. We take a little refresher course on the bunny slope. All the four-year-olds with balloons on their helmets fly past me, but I finally get the hang of turning and braking, and we decide I'm ready for the beginner slopes, the green slopes.

Kevin: "Want to go for it? Head all the way to the top and

make our way down?"

Me (*squinting up the mountain, feeling anxiety swirl in my gut*): "Um, how about we get off at the halfway point? I don't want to start off too fast like last time."

We get off halfway up. The snow is slushy and the area where we disembark the lift is wide and flat, so I have plenty of time to get myself ready to ski. Time to look down and see how ridiculously high up we are, because Canadian mountains are a gazillion feet higher than North Carolina mountains. Time to study the angle of the slope. Time to remember the statistics I once read about how many people die on ski slopes each year from hitting their heads on rocks hidden underneath the snow. Time to recall those awful ski blooper videos where people fly off slopes and end up a pile of mangled limbs in bloody snow. Time to ponder the four children I left back home with my in-laws. Four children who really enjoy having a mother who is (a) alive, and (b) in full possession of all four limbs. The swirling in my gut amps up to a small tornado.

Kevin (*punching me on the shoulder with an excited grin*): "Are you ready?"

Me (*barely whispering*): "Yes."

I shove off. If you know anything about skiing, you know that you're supposed to go downhill making big S-shaped curves to slow yourself down. You also know that beginning skiers brake by making a "snow plow"—pointing the tips of their skis toward each other in an upside-down V-shape.

I start down the slope, snow-plowing in the tightest S-curves imaginable, till I'm inching forward in tight looping curlicues— sometimes making full circles. All. The. Way. Down. The mountain.

It takes me a thousand hours to get down.

I wish I could say I got braver from there, that Adrenaline Junkie Elizabeth made her rip-roaring return, and Kevin and I zipped down the mountain together in romantic bliss for days. . .but I didn't. Honestly, I cried my way down several slopes, begging God to get me home safely to my sweet babies.

What was so different that second time? My life was different, and so was I. I had lived a lot more life in the past thirteen years. I knew too much. I had seen more injury, heard more horror stories. I had experienced a waterskiing accident that had injured my back and left me aware of my own limitations. I had children now—I wasn't just risking my own neck out there; I was risking four small people's mother. Thirteen years of living later, it was so much harder to be brave.

Isn't that the way life goes? When we are young and blissfully ignorant of some of life's hard things, less aware of our own frailty and limitations, convinced that "everything just works out when you love Jesus," how much easier it is to be brave, how much easier it is to go all in.

The older we get, the more we have lost. We have fallen and failed. We have hurt and been hurt. Seen death, known grief. Felt injury, disappointment, betrayal. Whatever griefs we have not experienced firsthand we have watched loved ones endure. We know life doesn't always work out with happily-ever-after endings, even for people who love Jesus.

The older we get, the more we have at stake. As time passes we accumulate things: achievements, passions, *stuff*. The more we have, the more we have to lose.

And it's not just things we accumulate; it's also relationships. The older we get, the more people we know—and love. The more we love, the more we risk. When we make sacrifices and hard choices for Jesus later in life, we're not just risking ourselves; we are also putting the people (and things) we care about at risk too.

And so we learn to keep our heads down. Live carefully. Stay safe. Put up fences and walls, safe borders.

God Keeps Calling, All Our Lives

Have you been brave for God in the past? Have you gone all in before. . .but somewhere along the way you took a step back? Have you pulled a Mary and pulled back your heart—forgotten your role, lost your way? Stepped in to pull God aside, to whisper in His ear, "Hey, this isn't the plan—this isn't what You promised me. Let's go back home."

Have you pulled a Peter and leaped out of the boat. . .but then as soon as you saw the wind and felt the waves, you clambered back to safety, soaking wet and soaked in shame, because Jesus or no Jesus, what kind of idiot tries to walk on water?

Just take a minute to ask yourself, "What would it look like if I went all in again? If I gave Jesus everything again? What would it look like if I was brave again at *this* stage of my life?"

Would you finally have the conversation you've been avoiding with your friend, your boss, your spouse, your child?

Would you stop worrying about what people think and start sharing your faith at school, at home, at work, in your neighborhood?

Would you open up with a trustworthy friend about the sin that's been dogging you—weighing you down, plaguing you with guilt, robbing you of peace and joy—and ask for prayers, for encouragement, for accountability?

Would you unlock the door guarding your heart and let people in—in where it's cobwebbed and messy, but in where it's honest and *real*? In where you love people as hard as you can, and when they love you back it's glorious, and when they hurt you it feels like a deathblow?

I am writing in Starbucks, wrecked over these words, because I need them as much as anyone. Too many times has fear kept a stranglehold on my life. Too many times has fear imprisoned my words. Too many times have I given God less than my best because I was afraid of being hurt. Too many times have I huddled down in the boat, safe from the storm. Still alive, still faithful, but not walking on water. No, I haven't drowned, but people can die in boats too.

When You Have to Find a Whole New Brave

Sometimes we have lost our courage and need to find it again; sometimes we need to find a whole new brave. A brave we have never needed before—and never wanted to need.

Lori sits at her kitchen table—it's buried beneath piles of receipts and tax forms—and weeps. She bought this table thirty years ago with her husband Brad. (We first met Lori in chapter 5.) They raised their family around this table. It has hosted thousands of cereal bowls, peanut butter and jelly sandwiches, and deep talks. Here the kids' hearts turned to Jesus. Here Lori and Brad stole kisses over coffee. And then Brad died. Left for a run and never came home. And here Lori sits, newly widowed, trying to do her own taxes for the first time in her life.

Lori has served God all her life, has done hundreds of brave things for Him with Brad over the years—moved her family around, risking their happiness and relationships in order to serve God in new places, but this—taxes, taxes *alone*—somehow feels like the bravest yet. Just one of a thousand things she is forced to do for herself and by herself, all while grieving the man she has loved since girlhood.

Every morning Lori opens her eyes to an empty side of the bed, and every morning it tears open the wound in her heart—the husband hole, the widow's scar. Every day she faces a host of reminders, new difficulties, insults to the injury of loss: toilets to unclog, grass to mow, hard-to-reach back-of-dress zippers to zip, and now—taxes.

And Lori has to find a whole new brave. A brave she never wanted to find. A kind of courage she never thought she would need. The courage to live alone, to live again.

We Are Not Alone

Alone as Lori feels, she is not alone in this. The Bible is filled with stories of men and women who lost their courage somewhere along the way, who faced challenges they had never imagined and then had to find a whole new level of courage to make it through. Think about Moses, Esther, Jeremiah. . .we could list names all day. So many of the people we admire in scripture had to find their brave not just once, but many times.

When I was young, it never occurred to me that I would face fear as a grown woman. I thought I would have life figured out by the time I hit the decrepit age of thirty. By forty (when I would surely be only a few steps away from blue hair and purple hats), all my major life battles would have been won and I could just nap my way through what little life remained until they forced me into a nursing home. How wrong I was!

Finding courage isn't just a young person's game. It's not something you master once and never face again. No, finding courage is a lifelong pursuit. The older we get, the more vulnerable and weak we may feel. The older we get, the more we have to risk; the older we get, the more we have to lose.

Borrowing Bravery: Using Your Past to Fuel Your Present

Have you ever noticed how many times in the Bible God calls His people to remember? *Reminds* us to remember? He even builds remembrance into our lives and our worship.

> *"But watch out! Be careful never to forget what you yourself have seen. Do not let these memories escape from your mind as long as you live! And be sure to pass them on to your children and grandchildren. Never forget the day when you stood before the* LORD *your God at Mount Sinai, where he told me, 'Summon the people before me, and I will personally instruct them. Then they will learn to fear me as long as they live, and they will teach their children to fear me also.'"*

DEUTERONOMY 4:9–10 NLT

And he took bread, gave thanks and broke it, and
gave it to them, saying, "This is my body given for
you; do this in remembrance of me."

    In the same way, after the supper he took the cup,
saying, "This cup is the new covenant in my blood,
which is poured out for you."

Luke 22:19–20

When it's time to find courage for a new stage of life, or time to find a whole new kind of courage, let's start moving forward by looking backward. Finding faith for the future by borrowing from the past. I don't mean looking back and saying, "Wow, I wish I could go back to the good old days"—no. Let's look back and remember times when we've been brave before, and it was worth it. Times when life was difficult but God saw us through.

And then let's look beyond our own lives, outside our own stories, past our own narrow perspectives. Let's look to friends who have seen spiritual victories through hardship. Let's look to the lives of God's people in scripture, recalling times when they faced challenges—maybe even lacked courage—and God gave them strength. God gave us their stories to encourage us, to strengthen our faith (Romans 15:4).

And then let us remember:

If God was powerful enough then, He is powerful enough now.

If God was wise enough then, He is wise enough now.

If God was kind enough then, He is kind enough now.

If God was faithful then, He will remain faithful now.

If God helped us to be brave once, He can help us to find bravery again.

Here's an exercise that will change your perspective if you need to find fresh courage: Take some time to think through your life and (don't panic, math-and-science people, I promise this won't hurt) do some writing. Jot down a description of the scariest times in your life and how you felt God's presence in those situations.

He may not have delivered you *from* those situations, but if you are alive today, then He has delivered you *through* them. Write down some of the specific ways God has protected you, comforted you, rescued you, or given you the strength and encouragement to make it through a painful time. If you have never tried an exercise like this before, get ready to be blown away. Also to cry a lot. Because when we sit and intentionally think through God's action in our lives, something amazing happens. The ordinary fades, the "daily-ness" of life falls away, and we catch a tiny glimpse into the big picture. In these quiet moments of meditation, the heavenly reaches in to touch the earthly.

The Greatest Courage

We left Lori sitting at her table, crying over her taxes. But Lori is determined. She recites her theme scripture, Psalm 75:3: "When the earth and all its people quake, it is I who hold its pillars firm," and she tells herself, "Lori, the God who is smart enough and strong enough to hold the earth in place is smart enough and strong enough to help you do your taxes."

She sorts receipts and adds numbers until she can't stand it anymore. Then she jumps to her feet, bursts into tears, and runs laps around the kitchen, flailing her arms and sobbing. . .but after a while there is nothing left to do but sit back down at the table. Back down with the evil forms. Again she sorts receipts, adds numbers. Then she jumps up, flailing her arms and sobbing and running again, this time holding a phone as she cries to her son. . .but when the fit is over there is nothing to do but sit back down at the table. Back down with the same evil forms. And somehow, by the time sunset spills across the table, the forms are complete. Every number added, every blank filled. Lori's taxes are done. She stares at the completed papers for a moment then leaps to her feet, happy tears streaming, and takes another arm-flailing lap around the kitchen—this one a victory lap: first taxes, now the world! Lori has found the courage she needs—a whole new courage.

We left Mary standing in the street, feeling betrayed by her son, wondering if she has lost Him forever. Probably angry with Jesus, definitely confused by God. Maybe searching her heart, desperate for courage. Did Mary go home and flail around her own kitchen table, a table Joseph had made her long ago as a wedding gift? Did she ponder the prophecies and come to a better (if still incomplete) understanding of her son's role? Did she get down on her knees and once more surrender to God her son's life—and her own? We don't know those things, but we do know that Mary came back—back to where the danger was, back to where she belonged—back to Jesus' side.

Once she returned, Mary stuck close to her son, so close she was with Him in His dying moments. No mother should have to witness such a horror—but how could Mary leave? Once again she had to find courage. Courage to stay. To keep watch, to bear witness, to weep over His last breaths. . .just as she once rejoiced over His first.

Mary's story shows us that none of us will be brave all day every day. In a lifetime of serving God, we will all fall prey at times to fear, to weakness, to insecurity. We will all succumb at times to doubt, to panic, to weak faith.

Mary teaches us that sometimes the greatest courage is in not giving up. In rising from weakness, daring to fight another day.

Sometimes the greatest courage is in strapping on skis with trembling hands, V-plowing down the mountain all the way to the bottom.

Sometimes the greatest courage is in flailing around the kitchen, tears streaming down, but then sitting back down at the table. Picking up the pen and filling in one blank, then another, then another.

Sometimes the greatest courage is in getting up after a fall, showing our face again to people who have seen us fail.

Sometimes the greatest courage is in sloughing off shame and regret—heavy weights, crippling chains—to stand tall in God's grace and say, "Here I am, Lord. Here I am to fight another day." Trusting that the God who holds the earth in His hands also holds *us* near His heart.

Let's Go Deeper. . .

For Further Study
God often called people to great sacrifice and courage later in life. Here are a few examples: Noah (Genesis 6), Abram and Sarai (Genesis 12:1–9), and Caleb (Joshua 14:6–14).

Journal Prompt
1. What are the bravest things you have ever done in your life? How did God help you through those situations?
2. In what new areas of life do you need courage?
3. Let's try the journaling suggestion on pages 128–129: Jot down a description of the scariest times in your life and how you felt God's presence in those situations. Now, in what specific ways has God protected you, comforted you, rescued you, or given you the strength and encouragement to make it through a painful time?

Prayer Prompt
Be my rock of refuge,
> *to which I can always go. . . .*
For you have been my hope, Sovereign LORD,
> *my confidence since my youth.*
From birth I have relied on you;
> *you brought me forth from my mother's womb.*
> *I will ever praise you.*
PSALM 71:3, 5–6

8
When God's
Call Is Unclear

Samuel's Story

Based on 1 Samuel 3

Samuel lies in his cot watching a dying flame, the lamp of the Lord. When he cracks open the door to his tiny room in the temple, he can watch the lamp all night long—and it can watch over him. His eyelids grow heavy, his blinks stretch long. The flame blurs, then twins, then melts back into one.

Even when his eyes drift close, the light sways against his eyelids, as if it hears a lullaby—the song of God, the voice of God. In his memory, Samuel hears Eli's raspy voice, just this afternoon: "The voice of God—oh, to hear it again."

"But Eli," Samuel had said, placing his young hand atop his mentor's wrinkled one, "you are still His prophet. You teach me His words."

"Thank you, my son." Eli's milky eyes crinkle down at Samuel. "The day is coming when *you* will be God's voice to His people—He will speak to you, and you will speak to them. You are nearly thirteen; we must get you ready."

Samuel's stomach gives a funny flip, part fear, part awe. His eyes flick to the curtain at the back of the tabernacle. Behind that curtain is the ark of the covenant, the golden chest that houses the Ten Commandments, Aaron's staff, a jar of manna—and the Spirit of God. Samuel has touched the curtain once—only once—a year after his mother brought him here to live with Eli.

Four-year-old Samuel tiptoes toward the curtain. Eli has used his mean voice to say, "Never go near it! Never touch it! God lives back there!" but today the curtain—purple and red and gold and alive—is all Samuel can think about.

Sunlight bounces off the golden threads like little pieces of fire—is it hot? The heavy fabric moves back and forth, like breathing; is God standing behind the curtain?

Maybe God will smile at me, he thinks, with a wondering thrill.

As if in a trance, Samuel tiptoes forward, chubby fingers outstretched. He just wants to feel it. Rub it between his fingers. Maybe take one tiny peek behind the curtain to wave at God, quick as lightning. He won't sneak behind the curtain; he knows better than that. His fingertips brush the curtain.

"Samuel! Samuel!"

Samuel's hand jerks back as if burned. He spins around. Eli is running through the tabernacle, his usually gentle face crooked and angry. Eli skids to his knees at Samuel's feet and grips his shoulders hard. Up close Eli's face is blotchy and his eyes are scary.

Eli gives Samuel a rough shake. "Didn't I tell you never, ever to go near the curtain, boy?" Eli shakes him again, a shake with every word. "If—you—touch—the—ark—you—will—die!"

Samuel's chest starts heaving. Hot tears rain hard. "I—wanted—to—see—Him," he sobs.

Eli's shoulders get smaller, his angry eyes turn nice again, and he takes his hands off Samuel's shoulders.

"Mama, Mama," Samuel cries, suddenly missing the soft hands he hasn't felt in so many months, the face he now remembers only in pieces, pieces he can no longer put together into a whole picture—dark hair, happy eyes, pink mouth. He slumps to the floor, spilling warm tears on cold stone. "Mama, Mama."

A hand rests gentle on his back. The hand makes circles—again Samuel thinks of Mama—and after a long time the circles help his breathing slow. After a while, strong arms lift him off the floor and fold him into Eli's lap. Still hiccupping, Samuel buries his face in the old man's rough linen tunic, inhaling the sharp smell—the smell of the *temple—that always clings to the prophet's clothes.*

"I'm sorry I yelled," Eli says quietly into Samuel's hair. His voice sounds strange, kind of thick. "The Holy of Holies is not a place to play—not for children, not even for adults. You must always listen to me, my boy. The Lord is kind, but His temple is not safe for those who do not obey."

"Samuel! Samuel!"

Samuel's eyes fly open. The light is still dancing. How long has he been asleep? Surely not long.

Over his tunic he throws on his robe, the one his mother brought on her last annual visit. He imagines it still smells like her—her spices, her home. He lights a candle and picks his way down a darkened hallway to Eli's room.

Samuel knocks on the wooden door. "Eli?"

A shuffling sounds on the other side of the door. "Whayawan?" comes Eli's mumbling voice.

"I—" Samuel makes a confused face at the door. "Here I am. You called me."

"I did not call you, boy. Go back to bed."

Samuel shrugs at the door and walks back to bed. He blinks a few times at the light in the lamp—it still burns strong, stronger than usual at this hour.

Sleep falls quickly.

"Samuel! Samuel!"

Samuel bolts upright. He'd been having a dream, a dream about the curtain. Golden light spilled from the gaps at the edges—top, bottom, sides—as though the sun was rising behind it; the shimmering fabric began to melt, liquid gold. He reached for the curtain, it scorched his fingertips—

He bangs on Eli's door. "Eli? Eli!"

Samuel pushes the door open and steps into Eli's closet-sized room. The room is lit by moonbeams flooding in through a small window. Eli sits up in bed in a wrinkled tunic, gray hair sticking out like a fluffy, faded crown. "Are you all right, boy?" Eli says, squinting, reaching out two hands as if to check him for injury with one hand, fever with the other.

"I'm fine. You called me, so. . .here I am?" Samuel says, feeling foolish and confused.

Eli's squint softens into a tired half smile. "You are dreaming, boy. Go back to bed."

Samuel studies Eli for a long moment. Is the old man finally losing it? Or just talking in his sleep? Chewing his lip uncertainly, Samuel nods and backs out of the room. As he shuts the door he thinks he hears Eli chuckling.

Samuel climbs back into bed, heart still drumming. His eyes fix on the lamp of the Lord. *Strange. It should be out by now.* The flame stands straight, an arrow pointing to heaven. When he closes his eyes, the memory of the flame remains.

"Samuel!" The voice is insistent, urgent, nearly a shout. "Samuel!"

The boy throws himself out of the bed and sprints. Skidding to a stop, he throws Eli's door open, not even bothering to knock. "Here—here I am," he pants. "Are you all right?"

Eli sits up in bed blinking. A dozen emotions chase each other across Eli's face—confusion. . .a tremor of understanding. . .delight. . .pride. . .and finally a sort of wistfulness. He pushes himself to his feet and shuffles toward Samuel, hands outstretched. "My son, I did not call you. You are hearing the voice of the Lord."

"The—what?" Samuel's stomach falls to his feet.

Eli smiles behind his beard. "The Lord is calling you, son. He has a message for you."

Samuel stumbles back a step, afraid.

Eli steps forward and places his hands on Samuel's face. "Do not fear. Go back and lie down, and if He calls you, say, 'Speak, Lord, for Your servant is listening.'" He gives an encouraging smile.

A thousand questions crowd Samuel's mind, so many he can't pick one: *How will I know—? What do I say—? What do I do —?*

But he just takes a few deep breaths and nods. Eli lets go, and

Samuel backs away. From the doorway he looks back, seeking one more encouraging smile. Eli gives it—always, he gives it. Samuel hesitates, hand on the door, feeling that perhaps he should leave it open. Perhaps Eli wants to hear the voice of the Lord too. But Eli gives a sideways nod that seems to say, *Go ahead. Leave me.* Samuel shuts the door, leaving Eli standing alone.

On the walk back to his bed he feels everything—the air whisking beneath his bare feet, the chill seeping up through the stone.

Leaving his door open, Samuel makes himself lie down. He does not take off his mother's robe. His eyes lock on the lamp of the Lord, seeking a friend. It blazes tall, like a soldier saluting.

He hears something shuffle outside his door. His breaths come shallow and fast. He squeezes his eyes shut—*Am I allowed to look?* The room warms, making Samuel's skin tingle. The shuffling moves into the room—closer, closer—and Samuel senses a presence beside the foot of his bed.

"Samuel." The voice is soft now—familiar, inviting. Masculine, but with a gentleness that somehow reminds him of his mother. "Samuel." He hears a smile in his name, an invitation.

Samuel opens his eyes. A figure stands waiting in the darkness, and Samuel sits up. "Speak, Lord, for Your servant is listening."

∽

Samuel received a call from the Lord, but it took him awhile to hear it. To receive it. Samuel didn't know how to hear God's voice—didn't even recognize it—because he had never heard it before. Samuel needed the help of an old pro, the aging prophet Eli.

In the pages of this book we are exploring how to respond when God calls us to something new. When we must rise to meet challenges and changes we've never faced before. When God calls us to move, give, or grow—maybe even gives us a loving kick in the pants.

But what about the times when we can't figure out what God is calling us to do, where He wants us to go. . .or if He is even calling at all? What about the times when we lie awake listening but the room stays silent? Or the times when we stand in the fork with two paths (even three or four) stretched out before us, and each path looks equally inviting? Or the times when we can't tell the difference between a gut feeling that means something spiritual—and a gut feeling gifted to us by an unfortunate encounter with a late-night burrito?

As you read, you may be asking yourself questions like these:

- I think God is telling me to go somewhere, do something, make a change. . .but I'm not sure. How do I identify a call from God?
- I don't really want to do the thing I think God might be calling me to. How do I know God is the One calling? What if I'm just hearing the voice of my own guilty conscience or the voice of peer pressure?

This chapter is going to serve as a bit of a time-out from the rest of the book. The chapter in which we lay out some basic ground rules for hearing the voice of God, interpreting His will in daily life, and making choices. Because when we say—when I write—"God is calling," those are somewhat presumptuous words. I feel uneasy penning them, as well I should.

For example, as I write this book, several people I love are weighing difficult decisions, life changes that *could be* considered calls from God. . .or perhaps not:

One friend is considering adoption. Although she already has children of her own, a full house, part of her heart longs to give a lonely child a home. But then. . .she's not sure if adoption is best for her family. Is adoption a call from God she *has* to fulfill, or is it a personal desire she is free to pursue—or not pursue?

Another friend debates taking on a second job to make ends

meet. He has multiple options, but he already has a busy full-time job, and each opportunity carries its own risk, its own cost. Does God have an opinion on this?

Another friend is considering a breakup. He is a good guy, a stellar Christian—but she feels unsettled, unsure. Is the unsettled feeling God's way of telling her to break things off. . .or is it just cold feet from old baggage?

Several friends enduring infertility are anguishing over complicated decisions about what kind of treatment to seek, what measures to take. What does God think about Clomid and in vitro? Is He calling my friends to act or to wait?

Another friend wants—needs—to move to live near her children and grandchildren, but it will mean moving away from her aging father, an already fragile man. He won't be alone—he lives with family—but still. . .he will miss his daughter dearly. What is God's plan for my friend—and for her father?

Let's acknowledge a difficulty: it is almost impossible, outside the specific commands of God recorded in scripture, for a human to confidently tell another human: "God is calling you to. . .go into the ministry. . .take a new job. . .break up with your boyfriend. . .adopt a child. . .buy a house. . ." (or any one of a million practical decisions). God may in fact want a person to do those things, but we humble humans can't speak with divine authority in such areas. When it comes to advising one another on our individual callings and decisions, let's be careful with our language.

So when can we be confident that God *is* calling a person? The scriptures are filled with universal calls (you could also call them commands or expectations) that apply to all believers, and we can share those calls with one another with confidence. All Christians are called to love God with all our heart, soul, mind, and strength; to love our neighbor as ourselves; to serve the poor; to be devoted members of the body of Christ; and the list goes on. When in doubt, let us speak with humility and with words that reflect scripture.

So Where's My Personalized Life Plan?

Wouldn't it be great if God handpicked the perfect spouse for us and put a sign on them with our name on it? Then we would never waste any time dating bozos, no one would ever get their heart broken. . .and the country music industry would immediately disappear (that last part would be sad). What if at birth we all received a Personalized Life Plan from God, a detailed calendar with directions for all of life's milestones:

In May of your twenty-sixth year, you should marry So-and-So. (Helpful hint: Head to church and you'll meet him there!)

In June of your thirtieth year, you should start trying to get pregnant. (Helpful hint: You ovulate on day 14, and it will coincide with a power outage during a thunderstorm!)

But we don't get that, do we? Not even close.

Many Christians believe that God has every step of our lives already decided for us. Not only does He *know* everything that is coming our way, but also He has predetermined our every step for us. And while we don't want to take anything away from God's omniscience or omnipotence—God is all-powerful and all-wise, free to do whatever He wants, whenever He wants to do it, through whomever He chooses—the Bible also teaches that God has given His children a lot of freedom in making choices for ourselves (see Deuteronomy 30:11–20; 1 Corinthians 6:12–20; Galatians 5:13).

Like a wise parent, our Father has given us guidelines and parameters in which to live. Yes, some decisions He has already made for us: Murder when you're angry? Not an option. Sex when you're not married (even if you really love each other)? Not an option. (Of course, thanks to freedom, we can choose to violate those rules—but we are not supposed to, and we suffer consequences when we do.)

But in many of life's decisions, we don't get specific instructions. We get options. Which means something amazing. . .and empowering: *God trusts us to make a decision for ourselves.* His only rule? That we enjoy our free choice within His loving limits.

I love the way Haddon Robinson explains this in *Decision-Making by the Book*:

> God cares about the decisions we make, and
> certainly each decision confronts us with
> choices, some of which are ultimately better than
> others. . . . If we make our decisions within the
> boundaries of God's sovereign and moral will, we
> have a great deal of freedom.
>
> The question we should ask is no longer,
> "What is God's will?" Instead, the question is,
> "How do I make good decisions?" If we change
> the question, we change the direction of the
> answer.[1]

God has entrusted humans, His last and greatest masterpiece, with the gift, the honor, the privilege, of decision-making. He has created us to depend on Him for life and breath, for salvation and wisdom, but He has also given us freedom to choose our own path and to *align* that path with His ways and His will.

Which means. . .

We get to choose what to do after high school.

We get to choose to stay single; or if we want to marry, we get to choose a spouse. (Of course, they have to choose us too—that's the maddening part.)

We get to choose a career.

We get to choose a city to live in and a specific apartment or house to live in.

We get to choose if and when we try to get pregnant or adopt a child. (You'll note I said "*try* to get pregnant or adopt," because as years of infertility pounded into my poor battered heart, we don't get to control how and when those things happen.)

Does God have opinions on these decisions? Yes. If we marry, He wants us to choose a spouse who loves Him and who will make us better for Him, closer to Him. A spouse who will help us raise our children in His ways, if God has children in our future.

He wants us to be a light for Him in our schools, neighborhoods, and workplaces.

He wants us to use our finances wisely—to provide for our own needs and our family's needs, and to give generously to others as we are able. He wants us to give back to Him and avoid greed.

Is It Really a Call from God?

In this book we are exploring the lives of several people who received personalized calls and instructions from the Lord. They spoke to burning bushes (okay, it was really just the one bush), they visited with angels, they heard the very voice of God. Since you and I live in different times—a time when Jesus has already come, when the church and New Covenant have been established, and when God's written Word is readily available to most Christians—our calls from God will likely look and sound very different from theirs. We won't always be able to draw direct comparisons from the Bible to our own decision-making.

But before we write off our Bible predecessors' stories as inapplicable to modern life, let us note this: Even our Bible heroes sometimes received incomplete information. And a direct call from God was no guarantee of smooth sailing or an easy path. If anything, a call from God usually meant "Buckle up—your life is about to get extremely complicated."

So if you are reading this book and wondering if God is calling you to something new—a big decision, a life change—here are a few Bible-based principles to help direct your thinking and prayers:

Don't sit around waiting for a voice from heaven.

Let's talk about what to expect—and not expect—from God. Sometimes reading the Bible throws us off a bit in terms of our expectations. We see the way God related to some of our Bible heroes—angelic visitors! direct revelations! personal prophecies! meaningful dreams!—and we think we should receive the same kind of personal, detailed direction for our lives. Perhaps unconsciously, we find ourselves searching for that kind of guidance, and when we don't receive it, we feel lost, insecure, even paralyzed. We think something is wrong with us—or wrong with our walk with God.

Without diving too deeply into the theology behind all this, let's make a few observations. For starters, our Bible heroes did not have ready access to the Bible as we do. (Depending on which Bible character we are talking about, parts of the Bible—maybe even most of the Bible—were still being written!) They couldn't just grab their Bible off the nightstand or open the Bible app on their phone. Even once the Law had been written down, most God-fearers did not have daily access to it. They had to rely upon hearing it read aloud in public assemblies. It makes sense that in the absence of written law and ready access, God chose to communicate with some of our spiritual ancestors differently—at times directly.

And let's keep this in mind: even in biblical times, *not every God-fearer received a personal revelation from God*. In New Testament times, God usually stepped in only when His people were making Big Decisions for New Directions—and often those decisions had to do with evangelizing a large group of people or establishing new, big-picture policy for God's people (see Acts 10, when the Gentiles were welcomed into the church and the old Jewish food laws were altered). We *don't* see Jesus showing up to say, "Hey, Timothy, you should ask that cute Greek girl out on a date—she'd make a great preacher's wife!" or "Hey, Lydia, you should sell your purple cloth business and go into full-time ministry!"

Much as we long to hear it, most of us are not going to get a voice from heaven calling our name, giving us specific direction. I'm not saying it's impossible, but it's improbable—not God's typical method of communication now that we have the Bible. And honestly? We don't *need* individualized instructions from God, because we already have the words and will of God at our ready disposal. God seems to consider those words—the Bible—to be sufficient in providing us with principles to guide both our overall life direction and our daily decision-making.

Learn how to listen. (And turn off the noise.)

"Speak, Lord, for Your servant is listening." Samuel had to learn how to listen to the Lord. And while you and I may not hear His audible voice in the same way Samuel did, we can still listen.

Modern life is noisy. Too noisy. We can't carry on a single face-to-face conversation with another human without some kind of electronic interference:

Ding. (Someone has commented on your post! You must reply immediately!)

Ping. (Someone likes your picture! You should respond by liking their like!)

Ding. (A text message from a friend about their outfit.)

Ding. (Another text message from same friend about their outfit.)

Ding. WHY HAVE YOU NOT RESPONDED TO MY TEXTS WHAT IS WRONG WITH YOU I AM IN A CLOTHING CRISIS! (Angry emoji.)

Silence. (No one has liked your posts/pictures/stories for the past five minutes. Time to feel insecure and post something new so you can be validated.)

Ring. (This is the sound of the phone ringing. An actual human is on the line. This could cause extreme anxiety, because who wants to speak voice to voice anymore?)

I fear that life has become so noisy, so distracting, that we've forgotten how to sit still and listen.

As my wise friend Lara Casey Isaacson has written, "Turn off *all* the dings!"[2]

It is difficult to hear the voice of God when our ears, our minds, and our hearts are constantly pulled in five million directions by phones, by posts, and even by people. If you think you are being called to go somewhere or do something new for God, before you move ahead, take some time. Time to calm your spirit and still your mind. Time to examine your heart—your motives, your gifts, your needs. Time to lie still as Samuel did and pray, "Speak, Lord, for Your servant is listening."

Seek spiritual principles in scripture.

> *Your word is a lamp for my feet,*
> *a light on my path.*
>
> PSALM 119:105

Reading scripture is a key way we listen to God. It helps us understand His priorities and learn what pleases Him.

Scripture illuminates our path. When we shine biblical principles on our decisions, our path is made clearer. God's Word casts light on the potholes and boundary lines. Although scripture may not give us an exact answer—*Should I seek a new job? Should I get a master's degree?*—it can often provide us with healthy parameters.

For example, God may not tell us which job to take, but scripture gives us these principles:

Seek God first (see Matthew 6:33; 22:37). *So. . .will this job allow you to prioritize God?*

Don't be greedy (see Luke 12:15; 16:13). *So. . .would taking this job make you a lot of money but force you to compromise your integrity or family life for the sake of money?*

You get the idea. Scripture gives us boundaries and limits our choices (in a good way). When we do our best to live according to biblical principles, we can be sure that God is pleased with us and that we have His blessing no matter what we decide.

Pray for guidance.

> *Teach me to do your will, for you are my God;*
> *may your good Spirit lead me on level ground.*
>
> PSALM 143:10

We need to listen to God, but we also need to speak with Him. When we are making a big decision, it is both wise and biblical to set aside special time for prayer. We see this example numerous times in scripture: Before beginning His ministry, Jesus spent forty days alone with God. Before selecting His twelve disciples, Jesus spent a night alone in prayer. Before going to the cross, Jesus prepared Himself in the Garden of Gethsemane.

When I have a big decision to make, I ask God if He has a strong opinion on the matter, and if He does, to make it known. I ask Him to close doors on poor options and make bright the best path. I ask Him, in the words of Psalm 139:5, to "hem me in behind and before"—to keep me from walking off His path or even walking too close to the edge! I take comfort from Proverbs 16:1: "To humans belong the plans of the heart, but from the LORD comes the proper answer of the tongue." God is involved in our daily lives, and He pays special attention when we pray (Matthew 6:6–15; Exodus 3:7; Psalm 38:9).

I have friends who have been so serious about seeking God's guidance in choosing a college that they have prayed, "Lord, please help me to only get into the school where I will do the best spiritually"—and God has usually obliged.

Seek wise counsel.
The Bible is clear: godly advice is a good thing!

> *Plans fail when there is no counsel,*
> *but with many advisers they succeed.*
> PROVERBS 15:22 HCSB

> *Plans succeed through good counsel;*
> *don't go to war without wise advice.*
> PROVERBS 20:18 NLT

Seek counsel from spiritual people who know God's Word

and know you. They can help you sort through the feelings, keeping God and His principles in mind.

Don't let feelings be your guide.

I know. This goes against every Disney anthem we've ever heard: *Follow your heart! Dreams come true! Let it gooooo!*

This even goes against a lot of "theology" I hear casually tossed around from believer to believer. People say things like, "I just really felt like that was the right thing to do." "I knew in my heart that God wanted me to do that." "God told me I should do that."

(Whenever people say, "God told me. . . ," I find it helpful to learn what they mean by that. *How* did God tell them? Did they actually hear a voice? Did they read a scripture that prompted their decision? Did they see a "sign"? Did they get a strong feeling? Some of those options I would consider valid ways of hearing God's voice; others, not so much.)

We're going to take some time to draw out this point, because it's a biggie. Feelings are *a* factor in our decision-making, but not *the only* factor.

Far be it from me to pretend that emotions aren't real or don't matter. (My husband once called me a sprinkler, remember?) It's just. . .it's wise to be careful when it comes to feelings. Feelings are fickle. Feelings can be affected by everything from hormones, to caffeine, to lack of caffeine, to medications, to conflict, to Facebook feeds, to Kleenex commercials, to thoughtless comments from friends, to last night's dinner, to—no, I'm not kidding—the stage of the moon and the presence of cats. Feelings are an unreliable—even dangerous—way to gauge truth or determine the will of God.

We find a great example of the danger of following feelings in Samuel's later life. Saul has become king, and Samuel serves as his prophet and guide. When Samuel first anointed Saul, he told him, "Do whatever your hand finds to do, for God is with you" (1 Samuel 10:7). Saul had a lot of freedom to make his own choices and determine the direction of his kingship. But even within this freedom, he had some limits.

In 1 Samuel 13 we find Saul and his army waiting for Samuel to arrive and make a sacrifice on their behalf. Samuel is the only one qualified to make the sacrifice, and Saul knows this. But Samuel is running late, the army is scattering, and Saul starts panicking. Fearing total desertion by his army, Saul offers the sacrifice himself, and here's what happens:

> *Saul offered up the burnt offering. Just as he finished making the offering, Samuel arrived, and Saul went out to greet him.*
>
> *"What have you done?" asked Samuel.*
>
> *Saul replied, "When I saw that the men were scattering, and that you did not come at the set time, and that the Philistines were assembling at Mikmash, I thought, 'Now the Philistines will come down against me at Gilgal, and I have not sought the LORD's favor.' So I felt compelled to offer the burnt offering."*
>
> 1 SAMUEL 13:9–12

Do you see that last line there? "I felt compelled." Saul had a strong feeling that he needed to act, needed to bypass God's instructions and make the sacrifice. (Only priests could make sacrifices.) In Samuel's absence, Saul couldn't consult Samuel, so he consulted his own feelings, his own inner compass. The results were catastrophic:

> *"You have done a foolish thing," Samuel said. "You have not kept the command the LORD your God gave you; if you had, he would have established your kingdom over Israel for all time. But now your kingdom will not endure; the LORD has sought out a man after*

his own heart and appointed him ruler of his people,
because you have not kept the LORD's command."

VERSES 13–14

Saul's feelings contradicted a command from God. Saul's feelings lost him his kingdom. What can we learn from this?

Beware feelings that contradict the Word of God. Saul had already received God's instructions from Samuel (wait seven days) and from the Law of Moses (only priests can make sacrifices). You and I do not have access to Samuel, but we do have access to the Word of God. If your feelings ever countermand the written Word of God, do not listen to those feelings.

The strength of a feeling does not indicate truth. This was no passing whim Saul felt; it was a strong feeling. But it was strongly in error.

Decisions made in panic mode tend to be poor decisions. Sometimes we put time limits on decisions for good reasons; sometimes we are just being impatient. Proverbs 19:2 tells us, "Desire without knowledge is not good—how much more will hasty feet miss the way!"

If Saul had taken a little more time to calm down—if he had slowed down just a few hours—he wouldn't have made this mistake. Sometimes we all have to make choices in crisis situations, and if we make them with prayer and advice and our best understanding of scripture, we can be confident that God is with us. But if we can slow down and calm down, giving ourselves time to think clearly, pray thoroughly, and seek wise counsel, we stand a better chance of making the best decision.

God wants to help us make wise choices. Samuel was distraught over this turn of events, and his words communicate God's sorrow too. This is not the way God wanted things to pan out for Saul—He knew kingship would not go well for Israel; He had predicted it—but had Saul made better choices, his reign could have gone differently.

I'm not saying we should completely discount our emotions

when making decisions. God cares about our desires, and He takes them into consideration when making His decisions (see Exodus 3:7; 1 Samuel 8:6–9; Isaiah 38:5). But our feelings should be only *part* of the equation, not—as we like to say in theology circles—the whole enchilada.

Thankfully, our wise Father has given us some reliable ways of discerning how He feels about things. He has given us His Word. He has given us examples of godly and ungodly people in scripture and in life—people who have made wise decisions and people who have made foolish ones. He has given us friends and family to advise us. He has given us prayer and the Holy Spirit.

Don't look for signs.

My cereal spelled out a word!

I drove past a billboard that said, "Go into all the nations"—it's a sign that I should be a foreign missionary!

The light turned green just as I thought about trying to get pregnant! I got a literal green light from God!

I have heard a lot of Christians employ what basically amounts to Christian superstition in their decision-making. My friend Jessica once begged God for guidance as she tried to decide whether or not to enter nursing school. With the deadline for fall enrollment looming, she felt intense pressure to make a decision, to hear the voice of God, immediately. After one particularly passionate prayer session in which she begged God to show her what to do within the next two days, she got up from her knees and went out to run errands.

At the first store, she spotted several nurses walking around the store. *Weird,* thought Jessica. She got in line and, lo and behold, she was standing in line behind another nurse. *Even weirder,* thought Jessica. She drove across town to run her next errand, got in line again, and froze, heart pounding. She was standing in line behind the same nurse from the last store! *This is too bizarre to be a coincidence,* she thought. *This must be the sign I've been praying for. God is telling me to go to nursing school.* She went home and sent in her down payment that same night.

Two months later, Jessica was rocking her classes with a 99 percent in chemistry—see? the same-nurse-in-line-twice sign was proving right!—but then Jessica got horribly sick. So sick she had to drop out of school in the middle of the semester. She never went back.

Instead, after a long and winding road with several false starts, dead-ends leading to U-turns, and several more detours down side roads, Jessica ended up working in publishing, helping to sell books that shape people's hearts and lives.

So what was that whole thing with the nurses that day? Jessica now realizes it was nothing more than coincidence. She saw what she wanted to see. With nursing school on her mind, desperate to see a sign from God, she was hyperaware of nurses everywhere she went. She felt pressure to make a fast decision, so she read divine messages into daily circumstances—messages that simply weren't there.

We do not serve a vague God. If God has a strong opinion about what you need to do in a certain situation, He is powerful enough to find a way to speak *clearly*—through scripture, through advisers, or by opening or shutting a door.

Give yourself permission to make a decision.

But that leads us to our next principle: If God leaves you with two (or more) options—all open doors, the pro-con lists ending in a dead heat, no clear "best decision"—then it's safe to assume He is leaving the choice up to you. He is your loving Father and He will be with you, cheering you on and supporting you, whichever choice you make.

Sometimes we sit around in indecision forever, afraid to make a choice because we aren't confident we know God's will. We grow insecure, tentative, even paralyzed. Fear reigns. We are so afraid of making a wrong choice, of misinterpreting the will of

God, that we do nothing. We sit around seeking signs—*absolute heaven-sent clarity*—and in so doing we abdicate responsibility for our own lives.

Give yourself permission to make mistakes.

When we live full lives, bold lives, lives not hamstrung by fear, we are going to make some decisions that are less than perfect— decisions that either don't play out the way we had hoped or that later we realize were not the wisest choice after all.

As Os Guinness puts it in his book *The Call*:

> In many cases a clear sense of calling comes only through a time of searching, including trial and error. And what may be clear to us in our twenties may be far more mysterious in our fifties because God's complete designs for us are never fully understood, let alone fulfilled, in this life.[3]

Samuel's life gives us a fascinating example of how God deals with us when we make poor decisions. For generations, God Himself ruled Israel. But the Israelites wanted to be like other nations, ruled by a human king. The people kept begging, "Give us a king!"; God kept insisting, "A king is a horrible idea!" But finally, during Samuel's time as judge, God gave in (see 1 Samuel 8).

But do you know what I adore about our gracious God? He stuck with His people even though He didn't like their choice. He still loved them, still paid attention to them, still tried to guide them through the minefield they had laid for themselves. He even replaced King Saul with a better option (David) when Saul lost his way.

God doesn't abandon us just because we make imperfect decisions. Just as a good parent loves and supports and encourages a child through a difficult season in life—even if that season is self-inflicted and ill-advised—so God does not leave us alone, even when we make a less-than-best choice.

Don't misinterpret hardship as condemnation.

When a decision brings difficulty or heartache into our lives, does that mean we have made a bad choice? Maybe. Maybe not. Sometimes life is just hard no matter what we do. No matter what we choose. Sometimes we find ourselves caught between the proverbial rock and hard place, and the best outcome we can hope for is "not horrible" (aka "not being squished").

We see this concept at work in the lives of our biblical ancestors: obedience and sacrifice for God often brought difficulty, pain, and loss into their lives. But no one would suggest that their obedience was a wrong decision! Let us be careful not to misinterpret misfortune as a sign of God's disapproval.

Jesus spent a night in prayer before choosing His twelve disciples, and one of the people He chose ended up betraying Him to His death. Had Jesus made a wrong choice with Judas? Had Jesus misinterpreted the will of God? No! Judas's betrayal and Jesus' suffering were a part of God's plan—His plan to save humanity. His plan to save you and me.

Sometimes the path of righteousness leads us not to quiet waters but through the valley of the shadow of death (Psalm 23:4 KJV). We are not promised escape from the shadows, but enough light to find our footing. We are not promised freedom from trouble, but strength to survive whatever trouble comes.

I once knew a girl who married a man she thought was godly, faithful, and trustworthy. Ten years and three kids later, she discovered he had been living a lie, cheating on her promiscuously. Was his unfaithfulness a sign that my friend had made a poor choice? Was this misfortune somehow her fault, God's way of saying, "You chose wrong"? Of course not. God limits our knowledge of future events. It is not our fault when people change. When *they* choose to do wrong. Just as God does not control us, so we do not control other people. And this exposes us to risk and to hurt that God would not have chosen for us.

But God has been faithful to my friend even through her loss. She has found happiness in a new marriage. She has found a faithful man to love her. A man to love her children. A man to stand in the gap left by the man who left them behind.

∞

As a boy Samuel learned to hear the voice of God. For the rest of his life, Samuel communicated God's words—and heart—to Israel:

> *The LORD was with Samuel as he grew up, and he let none of Samuel's words fall to the ground. And all Israel from Dan to Beersheba recognized that Samuel was attested as a prophet of the LORD. The LORD continued to appear at Shiloh, and there he revealed himself to Samuel through his word.*
>
> 1 SAMUEL 3:19–21

You and I may not hear the audible voice of God the way Samuel did, but we can still hear His voice through His Word. As we follow His call, let us seek His ear, His heart, and His presence. As we make choices, let us trust that our loving Father goes with us, before us, and behind us—that He is with us wherever we go.

Let's Go Deeper. . .

For Further Study

I quoted two great books in this chapter, *The Call* by Os Guinness and *Decision-Making by the Book* by Haddon W. Robinson. I recommend both as thought-provoking reading!

Journal Prompt

1. What decision do you most need guidance for right now? What

scriptures can guide you in making that decision, and who can advise you?

2. What intimidates you most about making big decisions?

3. Have you ever made a less-than-perfect decision but seen God make lemonade out of your lemons? Write about that time.

Prayer Prompt

Let the morning bring me word of your unfailing love,
for I have put my trust in you.
Show me the way I should go,
for to you I entrust my life.

Psalm 143:8

9
When Your Call Isn't Glamorous

Jonathan's Story

Based on 1 Samuel 17–18:4

"Jonathan, *wait!*" His father's voice. A king's command.

For once Jonathan does not obey. At the entrance to the commanders' tent, he half turns to call back, "I'm sorry, Father, but if you won't let me fight, I must at least go down there with my men. I cannot hang back safe with you—" He falters, watching hurt, then rage, flash across Saul's face. Jonathan shakes his head. "I have to go." He sprints away, feeling his father's anger follow him like a weighted shadow.

Skidding down the dusty hillside, he weaves through the army—once his men see his royal robe, they step aside and make a path. He emerges at the front of the line facing an open field, an expanse of dirt. Dead, dry land. On the other side of the valley, he sees the enemy line, smudged by distance and dust. Philistine armor glints gold in bright sun.

Two figures circle each other. Low to the ground, weapons drawn, puffs of dust rising with every footstep till they seem to dance in a brownish mist.

Jonathan's eyes, honed for war, trained to direct and oversee battles, scrutinize the warriors' movements. He misses nothing.

The giant—Goliath, they call him—moves with slow feet. His sword lists a bit to the left, his grip loose and lazy. But Jonathan is not fooled. The casual stance belies a deadly ferocity Goliath can unleash in an instant. The giant makes a show of breathing on his sword, shining it on his tunic, then flexing his muscles and gazing at his reflection in the blade.

Philistine laughter drifts across the dusty field.

Jonathan's men rumble disgust at the insult.

But the small one, the shepherd boy, David—he is everything Jonathan trains his warriors to be: Relaxed and ready. Up on his toes in a soft crouch. Coiled, taut, ready to release at the right moment.

The odds tell one story; Jonathan's heart tells another. The champion Goliath should win. The shepherd boy David will be slaughtered. *And yet. . .*

The giant gives a clumsy, halfhearted lunge forward; the boy springs back like a startled bird. The giant throws his head back, howling at the sky; Philistine laughter flies. The champion spins in a circle, bows to his men. They cheer. But Jonathan's eyes are on David as he pulls a stone from a pouch at his waist and fits it into the leather strap of his sling. Goliath makes a slow, indolent turn, and Jonathan notes the moment Goliath's eyes catch the movement of David's rotating wrist. His eyes narrow and his posture changes—every muscle alert. He starts slicing circles in the air with his sword—it whistles and glistens, an intimidating show.

But Jonathan's eyes are all for the boy: his wrist at his waist; the practiced rotations, the gathering speed. A smile starts at the corner of Jonathan's mouth.

The giant goes down into a crouch, eyes on the boy's wrist. Dance-like, David circles him, sidestepping and shouting, his hand a blur.

With a sharp snap of his wrist, the boy lets fly a stone. Goliath swings his sword. Air catches in Jonathan's throat.

The giant goes stiff—blood blooms bright on his forehead, a shock of red—then sags to the ground in a heap.

Two armies stand frozen.

In the unnatural silence David sprints forward and heaves the giant's sword into the air, staggering slightly beneath its weight.

The sword is nearly as long as David's body. With a howl he slashes it down on the giant's neck. The body gives a violent shudder. *Again*—blood sprays, a red geyser, the boy is soaked in blood. *Three times*. David flings the sword aside. He's breathing hard, he's covered in red. He bends over the body. With a savage roar he hefts Goliath's dripping head high. Spins a slow circle so both armies can see.

The world erupts. The Israelite soldiers give a cheer so loud Jonathan feels it vibrating through the soles of his boots. Jonathan throws his own arms up, adds his own voice to the noise. His face is wet, he's streaming tears, he's never seen anything—anything, *anyone*—so brave, so insane, so inspiring. And without knowing he's going to do it, he charges—his hand finds his sword and he's running, leaping over the body, chasing Philistines, following David.

Even when the battle fades, Jonathan cannot sleep. Does not want to sleep. Over and over he relives the scene: David's words ringing, confident and clear; David's wrist spinning, expert and sure; the army surging, possessed and inspired. David is no boy. He is a man—a man filled with the Spirit, a man after the Lord's heart, or so the whispers say. He is the man Jonathan longs to be. The man Saul should be. The man—so rumor says—Samuel has anointed to take Saul's place. *Jonathan's* place. And Jonathan knows what he needs to do. What he *wants* to do.

∞

Jonathan strides across the training field, interrupting the sparring. In his dust he leaves a line of soldiers standing at attention. None will move until he releases them. David, practicing with wooden swords against a man twice his age—and twice his size—spots Jonathan. Shoving damp red hair out of his eyes, David grins. "My lord," David says, placing his right fist against his heart and bowing.

"My *friend*," Jonathan corrects. He waves a hand, releasing

David from his submissive stance.

"So have you come to challenge my skill with the sword?" David juggles the wooden blade, tossing it back and forth with practiced hands. "Because I think I've become skilled enough to take you now."

Jonathan laughs. "I doubt that. . .but that's not what I've come for."

"No?" David points the sword at the bow and quiver strapped across Jonathan's chest. Lifts one mischievous eyebrow. "Shooting practice?"

"Hush," Jonathan says. "I'm here for something serious." He feels the army's eyes watching them—scores of soldiers. Just the way he planned it.

"Oh," David says, lowering the sword and the eyebrow, still half smiling. "As you wish." He drives the blade into the dirt and crosses his arms with a mock solemn expression.

Slowly, deliberately, Jonathan unbuckles the belt that holds his sword. The sword is a family heirloom—for show, not for fighting. Gathering the belt and sword into both hands, Jonathan lifts them high overhead to make sure all the soldiers see, then holds them out to David, palms up. "David, son of Jesse," he says, bowing his head, "I offer you my sword." David stares, mouth falling open as if he plans to object.

Jonathan gives his head a tiny shake no. David snaps his mouth shut. Eyes bright, face red, David ducks his head and reaches out for the gift. Jonathan closes David's hands around the sword and belt then reaches back to remove the bow and quiver from his back. Places them atop the sword in David's hands.

"Jonathan," David whispers, shaking his head, eyes glinting tears, "I can't."

"Take them, brother," Jonathan says, his throat tight around the words. A smile tugs at his lips. "Slay giants."

David bows and starts to step back, but Jonathan catches his wrist. "Wait." With an ache in his throat, Jonathan reaches to loosen the clasp at his neck, removing his robe—his *robe*: gold-threaded, resplendent, bearing the family seal. The robe everyone—the Israelite army, even the Philistine army—would recognize from afar. The emblem of Jonathan's authority, his inheritance, his future as king.

His memory flashes him back to the day his father stood him on a dais and placed the robe on his shoulders with all the army watching. As Saul leaned in to kiss his son—once on the right cheek, once on the left cheek, once on the forehead—the entire army had dropped to one knee. Jonathan had fought his tears then; now he lets them fall—but they are not tears of sorrow. They are. . .complicated, bittersweet, beautiful. Tears of fierce affection, brotherly love. Tears of gratitude for a friendship he had not expected to find, had not even known he'd been searching for. Tears of surrender to God's will, and—yes—a pang of loss for the life that might have been, the life his father had planned for him. But this is right. This is God's will—for David and for Jonathan. *He must become greater,* Jonathan thinks. *I must become less.*

Jonathan holds high the robe, pivots slowly to be sure everyone can see—soldiers' faces spin past, silent, surprised—and then he turns to David and places it on his shoulders. Ties the clasp at his throat. Just as his father had once done for him.

David makes a choking sound, but Jonathan is not done. He pulls his tunic over his head, placing it on top of the weapons in David's arms. He leans in to kiss David—right cheek, left cheek, forehead—and steps back. "*Lead*, brother. You will be king, and I will be second to you. It will be my lifelong joy and greatest honor." Jonathan drops to one knee. All is silent but for the sound of David's tears.

∽

Raised a prince, groomed to lead, trained for war: Jonathan was supposed to lead a glamorous life. A powerful life. A royal life. Like his father, Saul, the first king of Israel, Jonathan seems destined for greatness. Already his reputation for leadership and courage is well established: he and his armor bearer once took on a Philistine outpost, just the two of them, slaughtering twenty men in one crazy encounter. Their epic courage inspired the Israelite army to action, a rout. Jonathan is well on his way to becoming not just a good soldier, but a good king. Not just a good king, but a godly one.

But then a redheaded shepherd boy throws a rock, and everything changes. The plan Jonathan thought (actually, everyone thought) God had in mind for Jonathan's life turns out to be wrong. God doesn't want Jonathan to become king—He has another man in mind. Imagine the day Jonathan realizes this truth. Is he tempted to feel jealous? Resentful? Insecure? Discouraged?

But the thing is, Jonathan already loves David. Loves him like a brother. And so he steps aside.

∽

We tend to picture a call from Almighty God as some grandiose, glorious exploit—slaying a giant, saving the day—and sometimes it is. But sometimes God calls us to do quiet things. "Small" things. Step-aside things.

When we study the lives of men and women called by God in scripture, we see that their callings usually brought more difficulty than celebrity. More pain than fame. I say that not to discourage us from answering God's call, but to help us adjust our expectations and motivations. To encourage us when our gifts, our role, and our call are different than others'—or different than what we may have envisioned for ourselves.

Answering God's call means embracing the way of Jesus: the way of humility, sacrifice, and service. Giving up yourself, your place, your rights:

> *Do nothing out of selfish ambition or vain conceit.*
> *Rather, in humility value others above yourselves,*
> *not looking to your own interests but each of you to*

the interests of the others.

>*In your relationships with one another, have the*
same mindset as Christ Jesus:
>>*Who, being in very nature God,*
>>>*did not consider equality with God some-*
>>*thing to be used to his own advantage;*
>>*rather, he made himself nothing*
>>>*by taking the very nature of a servant,*
>>>*being made in human likeness.*
>>*And being found in appearance as a man,*
>>>*he humbled himself*
>>>*by becoming obedient to death—even death*
on a cross!

PHILIPPIANS 2:3–8

Centuries before Christ, Jonathan steps aside to allow his friend David to take his place as Israel's future king. Let us rethink and redefine what it means to "go" for God; let us reconsider what we expect from God in this life.

Behind-the-Scenes Takes Center Stage

Sometimes we celebrate too much the public, "center stage" gifts in the church: preaching, teaching, worship-leading. Sometimes we assume that full-time ministry is, if not the best way to serve God, at least the most meaningful way. *If only I could teach the Bible the way so-and-so does,* we think to ourselves, *then I would be useful to God.* Or *If only I could plan epic church events like so-and-so does, then I would be valuable in the church.*

When I was in high school and college, I half idolized the people who led up front at church: the preachers, the teachers, the worship leaders. I admired their hearts, their courage, their charisma—and, yep, I admired the up-front nature of their role. It all seemed so inspirational and exciting! *They* seemed inspirational and exciting.

How differently I see ministry now! Church is more—so much more—than the preachers, the teachers, the singers. Where my ministry heroes used to be the up-front leaders, now they are the behind-the-scenes workers, the servants without whom the minister would be overwhelmed and the church would fall apart.

Sherl is the volunteer coordinator of the children's ministry at our little church. When we send the children off to Sunday school class midway through our worship service, they all squeal with delight and skip to line up behind Sherl. We call her the Pied Piper.

Every quarter Sherl organizes teaching rotations of busy volunteers who sometimes forget they signed up, and she herself may fill in when they forget. Twice a week she lugs a bulging bag of Sunday school supplies in and out of our rental facility. Every week she designs lesson plans, makes copies. Fields questions and opinions. Buys crayons on sale. Hands out bandages for skinned knees. And in all of this, through all of this, Sherl instills a love for Jesus and His church into the heart of every child blessed enough to sit in class with her. She has done this for the five years since we have started our little church. She has done it quietly, with few accolades and no payment, out of love for the Lord and love for other mothers' children. By her sacrifice and service she has helped to inspire all the children in our congregation, mine included, to love Jesus. Before Sherl, my kids often cried going to the kids' class; now they cry if they have to miss. Our church recently saw our first "homegrown" high school graduate—Samaria, the oldest child in our church plant five years ago—give her heart to God and get baptized in the Atlantic Ocean. Sherl was there on the beach that day alongside Samaria's family, praising God and sharing their joy.

And then there is Sammy. Sammy is our church's volunteer "sound guy." Sammy, a DJ who often works till the wee hours on weekend nights, is the first person at church every Sunday after my husband unlocks the doors. Sammy spends several hours cracking jokes as he hooks up mics, sets up speakers, and tapes down wires for the worship team. When church starts, Sammy praises God all by himself from the crow's nest, where no one can see him. (No one, that is, but God.) The singers sing, the preacher preaches. . .but without Sammy, no one would hear a word.

I'm not down on public ministry at all—I am the daughter, wife, and sister of ministers, and I am a part-time minister myself. If you are called to public ministry, by all means, *go for it*! But if that is not your calling, please understand that there are many other beautiful gifts and essential roles to fill in God's church. Without the right people filling them, the church is left imbalanced and incomplete.

Glamorizing public ministry can do two unfortunate things in our hearts: it makes us aspire to service that may not suit our gifts, and it makes us downplay and devalue behind-the-scenes contributions—others' offerings as well as our own. As David wrote, "I would rather be a doorkeeper in the house of my God than dwell in the tents of the wicked" (Psalm 84:10).

Perhaps David first learned this lesson in humility from his friend Jonathan. Jonathan was no less gifted than David—no less a warrior, no less worthy. Even as King Saul falters, Prince Jonathan shines: selfless and noble, loyal and bold. Even so, God didn't call Jonathan to be king; He called David instead.

Quiet Gifts

Jonathan gave David his tunic, his sword, his bow, and his belt—symbolic gifts all—but that was just the beginning. He gave David his heart. His friendship. His devotion and protection even when they endangered Jonathan's relationship with his father—even when they endangered Jonathan's life (see 1 Samuel 20:32–34).

When David fled from Saul, again Jonathan risked his life to find his friend:

> *While David was at Horesh in the Desert of Ziph, he*
> *learned that Saul had come out to take his life. And*

*Saul's son Jonathan went to David at Horesh and
helped him find strength in God. "Don't be afraid," he
said. "My father Saul will not lay a hand on you. You
will be king over Israel, and I will be second to you.
Even my father Saul knows this." The two of them
made a covenant before the LORD. Then Jonathan
went home, but David remained at Horesh.*

1 SAMUEL 23:15–18

*"Jonathan went to David at Horesh and helped him find strength
in God."* To help a hurting friend find strength in God—what a
gift. Is there any greater? It was a gift David treasured always.

And note Jonathan's willingness to step aside, his gracious
acceptance of his own demotion: "You will be king over Israel,
and I will be second to you." Centuries later, John the Baptist said
something similar when the Messiah came along and drew larger
crowds than John: "He must become greater; I must become less"
(John 3:30). Sometimes we are called to step aside so that someone else might fulfill their calling—and this stepping aside is no
small thing. Our humility and graciousness can be a noble sacrifice, a holy offering. As Aaron and Hur held up Moses' arms—
literally held up his arms—so he might lead the Israelite soldiers
to victory (Exodus 17:12), so Jonathan supports his friend.

When I was in high school, my parents moved to a new city
to help rejuvenate a church that needed a boost. Normally when
a church hires a new minister, the old minister moves away. It
can be awkward—maybe even painful—to stick around watching someone else take charge of your life's work. But in this case,
the former preacher stayed. He loved his church so much that
he wanted to help ease the transition; he was not too proud to
step aside and help someone else lead the family he loved. I have
never forgotten his gracious example of selfless humility.

Quiet Service, Great Value

Do you realize that using our gifts for God is an act of worship? We honor God—we bring Him glory and praise, we celebrate His marvelous creation and honor His endless creativity—when we use the gifts He has given us:

> *And so, dear brothers and sisters, I plead with you to give your bodies to God because of all he has done for you. Let them be a living and holy sacrifice—the kind he will find acceptable. This is truly the way to worship him.*
>
> ROMANS 12:1 NLT

Giving ourselves to God—our bodies, our personalities, our strengths, our energies, our hearts, our talents—is an act of worship. This passage goes on to describe the different ways God gifts His people.

> *In his grace, God has given us different gifts for doing certain things well. So if God has given you the ability to prophesy, speak out with as much faith as God has given you. If your gift is serving others, serve them well. If you are a teacher, teach well. If your gift is to encourage others, be encouraging. If it is giving, give generously. If God has given you leadership ability, take the responsibility seriously. And if you have a gift for showing kindness to others, do it gladly.*
>
> VERSES 6–8 NLT

In his grace God has gifted us all. Our gifts are His grace. No gift is more valuable than another; they—and we—are all needed to build up God's church. If one gift is missing, the entire body of Christ suffers loss. As Paul puts it in his first letter to the Corinthian church:

The human body has many parts, but the many parts make up one whole body. So it is with the body of Christ. . . .

If the foot says, "I am not a part of the body because I am not a hand," that does not make it any less a part of the body. And if the ear says, "I am not part of the body because I am not an eye," would that make it any less a part of the body? If the whole body were an eye, how would you hear? Or if your whole body were an ear, how would you smell anything?

But our bodies have many parts, and God has put each part just where he wants it. How strange a body would be if it had only one part! Yes, there are many parts, but only one body. The eye can never say to the hand, "I don't need you." The head can't say to the feet, "I don't need you."

In fact, some parts of the body that seem weakest and least important are actually the most necessary.

1 CORINTHIANS 12:12, 15–22 NLT

Crooked Toes Matter

Have you ever felt like your gifts aren't as shiny as other people's? Like your contributions to your family, your workplace, your friends, or God's church all seem so. . .small? As Zechariah 4:10 says, "Who dares despise the day of small things?" God sees small things. He values them. As Jesus celebrated the two coins donated by the poor widow—all she had to live on—so God honors the humblest responses to His lofty call (Mark 12:41–43).

And let us not judge our worth based upon how our offerings photograph on social media. Let us not downplay the importance of small—even secret—contributions to God's work. Jesus promises, "Your Father, who sees what is done in secret, will reward you" (Matthew 6:4).

I have broken the fourth toe on my right foot at least twice, and jammed it so many times I've lost count. The first time it happened, I'm sorry to say, I broke it *on my toddler*. Wait—before you condemn me as a child-kicker, I can explain! We were walking side by side through the house, holding hands—I the wobbly pregnant woman, she the wobbly new walker—and somehow my right foot snagged on the back of her left ankle. *Snap.* Cataclysmic pain shot through my body from a tiny body part I had never spent more than fifteen seconds even thinking about before.

And that was just the first time. The poor battered toe is now the shape of a cashew nut, perfect for catching on furniture legs. . .catching, hooking, and spraining—or breaking—yet again. It is a vicious cycle, and over the years it has become a running joke in my marriage. Kevin can now recognize the exact shout I make whenever I jam or break that stupid toe. (I made the Injured Toe Shout both yesterday and today. I am not kidding.) He doesn't even bother to come running anymore; he just calls, "Did you break your toe again?" And then he, hard-hearted soul that he is, *laughs at me* and leaves me to stand there muttering at the carpet.

Back to the toe. Toes are tiny, seemingly insignificant parts of our bodies, and yet as I can testify—oh, how I can testify—when you have an injured toe, it affects your entire body. That tiny toe *matters*. Your walk is wrong; your gait is off. The whole body suffers pain. Even minor daily activities are no longer simple. If you limp long enough, you can even end up messing up your hips and spine.

Perhaps you feel like nothing more than a crooked fourth toe in the kingdom of God. You spend most of your time hidden. You do your work for the Lord encased in a sweaty sock, working alongside all the other toes. Every so often you get treated to a pedicure; every so often you get to show yourself off in an open-toe high-heel shoe—wow, do you feel fabulous on those days—but most of the time, you work out of sight, helping the body keep balance from inside your sock.

But you, my dear crooked toe friend, are just as important as all the other parts. When you rejoice, the rest of the body rejoices with you. When you are broken or injured, we feel your absence. We hurt when you hurt. Our walk is wonky without you. The entire body is affected by you—yes, you—no matter how invisible or damaged you may feel.

How Do We Identify Our Gifts?

We tend to underestimate our own gifts. We take them for granted because they come so easily. We assume that other people must also be able to do the same things as easily as we can. "Being outgoing isn't a gift," laughs the outgoing person. "Isn't everyone excited about a party? Doesn't everyone just *live* for befriending new people? Also *dancing*?" Um, no. Tell that to the introvert hiding at the punch table, sweating through her deodorant!

"Having people over for dinner isn't a spiritual gift," shrugs the hospitable person. "It's just what you do for people you love." Tell that to the girl who can hardly microwave popcorn for herself, let alone plan a nice meal for guests! Showing hospitality is both a Christian service and—for some—a spiritual gift.

"Making people feel loved isn't a spiritual gift," says the encouraging person. "It's just basic Christianity." Tell that to the person who struggles to connect and make friends, the one who tries to encourage people by saying awkward things like, "Wow, your hair doesn't look greasy today. Did you wash it?"

Don't dismiss or undervalue your gifts just because they come easily. Use them! Expand them! Enjoy them! Offer them to God to use as He wills. As Paul urges Timothy, "Fan into flame the gift of God" (2 Timothy 1:6).

Certainly, the fact that our natural gifts come easily should give us a sense of humility about them. We call them gifts because God *gave* them to us for our enjoyment—and His. We can't take credit for our natural aptitudes; we can only thank God for them and use them for His purposes and glory.

Before I start a day writing, I will often pray something like this: "Lord, take me and use me today. You have made me a writer, and today you have given me the great privilege of writing for You. Please fill me up and then empty me out. Speak to me, in me, and through me. Please take my views on scripture, my personality, my writing style, my sense of humor, my life experiences, my family, my childhood, my worldview, my mistakes and regrets and weaknesses—everything You have given me, all I have to give— and use it all for Your purposes. Use my head, my heart, and my hands to put words on paper that accomplish Your will. Give me the words, and I promise I will write them down."

How can you take *your* gifts and pray a prayer like that? "Lord, use my social media skills to encourage someone today. To build up the body of believers online. To serve my church. To be a light in a dark world." Or "Lord, I offer You my bubbly personality. Please use me wherever I go today to encourage people who are down— and more than that, to point them to You for hope." Or "Father, please take my knack for fixing things and use it for Your purposes. Please lead me to people who need help around the house. Please allow me opportunities to serve the church itself, to help individual believers, and to serve my neighbors and show them the selflessness of Christ." You see what I mean? Pray to find uses—godly uses—for your gifts, and watch what God does with you.

How do we identify our spiritual gifts? Here are a few diagnostic questions to ask yourself:

- What do you like to do?
- What do you naturally do well? What comes easily to you? (If you're not sure, ask your family and friends.)
- What are other people always asking you to do for them?
- What do you gravitate toward doing in your spare time?
- What do you often get compliments for doing?
- What would you do in the church—how would you serve—if you didn't care what people thought?[1]

Is a pattern emerging? Once you have identified your gifts, ponder this: How can you use those gifts for God? How can you use those gifts. . .to help a neighbor? To encourage a friend? To serve your church? To give to people in need? To bring light to your community?

Your role may not be glamorous, it may not be up-front, it may be quiet and behind-the-scenes, but if you use your gifts to serve God, then you are fulfilling your calling. Your heart will be full and your Father will be proud.

∽

Jonathan's life on earth began in a palace and ended on a battle-field. His part changed from starring role to supporting cast. Ever humble, ever noble, he accepted this change with grace. Jonathan did not seek honor in life, but how David honored his friend in death! David sang this song:

> *How the mighty have fallen in the thick of battle!*
> *Jonathan lies slain on your heights.*
> *I grieve for you, Jonathan, my brother.*
> *You were such a friend to me.*
> *Your love for me was more wonderful*
> *than the love of women.*
> *How the mighty have fallen*
> *and the weapons of war have perished!*
>
> 2 SAMUEL 1:25–27 HCSB

Jonathan's friendship won David's heart. His faith gave David strength. His humility gave David a future: he kept the nation from dividing loyalties between the old line of Saul and the new reign of David. And Jonathan's example lives on thousands of years later, inspiring us—calling us higher—as we also seek to follow God's call.

Let's Go Deeper. . .

For Further Study
You can read more about Jonathan in these passages: 1 Samuel 13:16–14:52; 18:1–5; 19; 20; 31; 2 Samuel 1. If you want to read how David remained loyal to Jonathan, still honoring their vows many years after his friend's death, read what David did for Jonathan's son Mephibosheth in 2 Samuel 4:4; 9. Prepare to weep.

Journal Prompt
1. Write down answers to the list of questions on page 169. Do you see a pattern emerging? What are your gifts?
2. What role do you think God wants you to play in His church? How do you feel about that role?

Prayer Prompt
Better is one day in your courts
than a thousand elsewhere;
I would rather be a doorkeeper in the house of my God
than dwell in the tents of the wicked.
PSALM 84:10

10
When God Says, "Stay"

Legion's Story

Based on Mark 5:1–20

*C*ome out of him!" Each word a thunderclap. Legion hears as through a tunnel, his ears no longer his own.

Fury rises. Hatred, violence, a churning swell. It blinds him, it binds him—tremors rack his arms, his legs—a rage so all-consuming it escapes in a murderous howl. He doesn't know where *they* end and he begins—their feelings, his feelings, *our feelings, we are many, we are one*—he's pinned beneath a towering wave, drowning. Losing what remains of the man he used to be: a man who was a boy, a boy who had a mother, a mother who called him by name.

He used to have a name. A name she gave him.

Words pour from Legion's mouth like vomit—curses, threats, vitriol. He shuts his eyes, the only resistance he can manage. He does not want to see the prophet's face as the insults seek home. But even blind he spills words, a caustic flood.

At last *they* dam the flow. He sags, he sways, panting and heaving. He waits, *they* wait—*we wait, we are many, we are one*—for the prophet's response. Giddy, they long for the prophet's anger, His disgust, for the hatred that feeds them. Their hunger sears Legion's throat, his veins, a desperate burn.

But the hateful response doesn't come. The hunger claws.

Legion opens his eyes. The prophet stands quiet, unmoving, staring them down.

The hunger, the rage, they twist into something else. . .something tasting of metal and blood. *We are outmatched. We are doomed.*

The voices inside begin to whine, childish and trembling.

His voice, *their* voice—*our voice, we are many, we are one*—begs for mercy. "Please do not destroy us, oh Holy One. Send us into the herd of pigs over there." They hurl Legion to his knees, make him grovel.

The prophet gives a slight nod. Legion feels their surge of relief, quickly overwhelmed by fresh thirst for new blood. Pig blood.

The prophet raises His hands, His voice, and shouts, "Now be gone! All of you! Come out of this man!"

A tornado tears through him. It steals his breath, it stops his heart. Sound roars through his body, his ears—five thousand moans of defeat, five thousand shrieks of bloodlust. One voice cries louder than the rest—haunted, feral, a death cry. On and on it keens, shredding his throat, searing the sky. He falls to the ground and rakes at his ears.

A warm hand closes around his elbow, shocking him into stillness. The voice stops screaming. Legion's throat stops burning, though an ache remains. His eyes open to meet eyes—*His eyes*. The prophet's eyes. Warm and brown and unafraid. Soft eyes, searching eyes, curious and maybe even. . .but no, he's forgotten the word.

In the silence, in the dirt, Legion realizes that the scream was his own.

He tenses, waiting for their voices to fill the void, resume their babble inside. But his head stays quiet—too quiet. Unsure, he stumbles to standing. He is hollowed, drained, an empty vessel.

The prophet points, and Legion follows his finger. A cloud of dust trails a stampeding herd, pigs past counting. Legion can hear squealing and screaming; he never knew pigs could scream. Watching them, hearing them, he feels a pang, a pain he cannot identify. The herd races down a steep hill and plunges into the lake. The water bubbles, roiling with writhing pink bodies.

Legion looks away from the lake, the dying, back to the prophet. Legion cringes, waiting for the man to send *him* running. . .into the water, where he deserves; into chains, where he has been so many times; into the cemetery, where he has lived for so long. Instead the prophet casts him a crinkle-eyed smile and bends in close to whisper, "Don't move, I'm blocking the view; Peter is bringing you a cloak."

Legion narrows his eyes, confused, and looks down at himself—with a jolt, he sees he is naked. He barely has time to take in his battered, bloodied limbs before they are covered by a rough brown robe that falls to his ankles. A bearded, broad-shouldered man loops a sash around Legion's waist, steps back, and flashes a smile. "Don't worry about getting it back to me."

Legion tries to remember the right words—he knows he should say something to the man—but he can't think. It's too quiet. Too long his thoughts have not been his own, and now he has lost the words, maybe even the feelings. Like the grave, he is ruin and bone.

He looks up, and the prophet shines a smile, warm sun after endless rain. "Look at you! All you need now is a bath and. . .a name?" The prophet's look is searching, as if He can read Legion's thoughts, sense his emptiness.

"I—" Legion casts back in memory, hits a blank wall, and feels something like despair—the loss of a name, the final insult. "I have been Legion too long." He hangs his head.

The prophet reaches out a hand to squeeze Legion's arm. "If you cannot remember before long, I will give you a name. Now come, John has found you a place to clean up. Tonight you dine with Me. My name is Jesus."

Days Legion spends at Jesus' feet, drinking in His words—words of hope, truth, new life. The prophet weaves tales of fathers and sons, of lost things found. Sometimes Legion listens, sometimes he weeps, and sometime in the third day, he remembers how to laugh.

Again time is lost; how long has he sat spellbound? Days, weeks, a month? But one afternoon a crowd rises on the hillside—angry pig farmers, anxious mothers. Voices rise and boats are called.

Jesus is leaving.

Legion stands paralyzed as Jesus' disciples shoulder packs and move toward the water, into the waiting boats. Panic spirals. They cannot leave him alone. Without Jesus to protect him, to fill him, who else—*what* else—will show up to occupy the vacant spaces? To bring words to the silence?

He elbows his way through the jostling crowd of laughing people—John, Peter, Andrew, a cluster of women—and catches Jesus at the water's edge. Lunging, Legion grabs a fistful of Jesus' cloak. "Please, Lord," he huffs, "wait. Take me with You. I will be useful, I will earn my keep, I will do anything, just—do not leave me alone."

That smile again. Stepping back from the boat, Jesus motions Legion aside, away from the crowd. Places a hand warm on his shoulder. "My friend, you must stay."

"Stay?" The word is a spear. Legion feels everything sink—shoulders, head, hope. "But I want—I wanted—to go with You. To be with You always."

Jesus nudges Legion's head up with a finger crooked under his chin. His eyes shine kind—*kind*, that's the word. "Stay here. Go home to your own people and tell them how much the Lord has done for you—how He has had mercy on you. How else will they hear of Me? And they must be missing you. You must tell your story—share what you have been given."

As Jesus speaks, Legion feels a spark inside, the smallest of flames. Small but insistent, already casting warmth and light. He senses that soon it will blaze large enough to fill his empty spaces, maybe even to light other lights. *Stay behind. Go home. Tell what God has done.* A purpose, a mission.

He looks behind him at the road snaking uphill toward home and then on to the Decapolis—ten cities filled with people who need what he has found.

Legion looks back at Jesus. Again comes the feeling that Jesus is reading his thoughts. With a sad half smile Jesus says, "Did you ever find your name?"

Legion shakes his head, blinking fast. "Lost to time. Lost to *them*."

"Try Zechariah," Jesus says. "It means 'whom God remembered.'"

His throat thickens. He cannot speak, cannot thank—*thank you*, at last he remembers the words—he only nods as Jesus claps a hug around his shoulders and steps back, soft-eyed and smiling, into the boat. Andrew and John give the boat a heave. They row for the horizon, laughter drifting back to shore, black silhouettes against crimson sky.

With a final wave—does he imagine it, or does a tiny arm wave back from Jesus' boat?—he turns to the shore.

"Hey, Legion," calls a man behind him, saddling a donkey. "I thought for sure you'd go with Him."

"I've decided to stay." He grins. "And please—call me Zach."

∽

Legion is all but lost. His mind and body overrun by demonic forces, he wanders among tombs, the dead his only friends.

But God. God shows up—Jesus comes to town—and in an astounding display of authority over all powers, human and hellion alike, He calls Legion back from the grave. In a foretaste of Jesus' victory to come, His future triumph over death and decay, Jesus calls Legion out of the tombs, back to life. We soon find Legion sitting at Jesus' feet, "dressed and in his right mind."

Legion's transformation from demoniac to devotee stands among the most dramatic before-and-after stories in scripture. I've always held a special place in my heart for Legion: his body overtaken, his name not his own; a prisoner trapped in his own mind, his own body. He is a physical embodiment of the struggle we all face with sin, Romans 7 incarnate: "The evil I do not want to do—this I keep on doing. Now if I do what I do not want to do, it is no longer I who do it, but it is sin living in me. . . . Who will rescue me from this body that is subject to death?" (verses 19–20, 24).

I too have fought internal battles: thoughts that would not be tamed, feelings that would not be chained. Any among us who have endured chronic emotional suffering—depression, anxiety, addiction, mental illness, eating disorders, self-harm—may find a friend in Legion. We may find hope in his healing, the assurance that there are no powers Christ cannot overcome, no chains He cannot break.

Legion clings to Jesus, finding himself by finding *Him*. He doesn't simply ask to go with Him on His missionary journey; he *begs*. Imagine the terror Legion must have felt at the prospect of being left alone without Jesus to guide him, left empty without Jesus to fill him.

We don't get many details about Legion's life after Jesus left, only this:

> As Jesus was getting into the boat, the man who had been demon-possessed begged to go with him. Jesus did not let him, but said, "Go home to your own people and tell them how much the Lord has done for you, and how he has had mercy on you." So the man went away and began to tell in the Decapolis how much Jesus had done for him. And all the people were amazed.
>
> MARK 5:18–20

Jesus asked Legion to stay behind because He had an assignment for him. A mission. Legion didn't *just* stay behind—he stayed behind and went somewhere: back home to his family and on into ten neighboring towns called the Decapolis. Legion told everyone who would listen what Jesus had done for him, and all who listened stood amazed. Ten cities heard about God's power and mercy because Legion stayed behind. Because Legion stayed home.

I don't want to give us the wrong idea with the title of this book, *When God Says, "Go"*—because sometimes God doesn't want us to go anywhere! Right now God may not be calling you to move to a new city or seek a new job or assume a new role. God always wants us to move forward, but that forward motion often happens right where we are, in the life we already have, among people we already know. Sometimes God tells us to go *and stay*:

Stay home.

Go back to an old place with a new attitude.

Show His grace to our family.

Share His love with our neighbors.

Go deep.

Love hard.

Grow strong.

Serving God isn't always loud and dramatic and full of transition; most of the time it's quiet. It's humble. It's simple. And it's hard work.

Have you been feeling bored and uninspired, twiddling your thumbs and waiting for God to say, "Go"? Waiting for Him to call you to something new and exciting? *I want to go for it for God, but first He needs to change my circumstances. . .* But consider this: Maybe God has *already* said, "Go!" Maybe He said, "Go," long ago when He put you in your current situation—but you got there and never really *went*. Your body arrived, but your heart stayed somewhere else. As soon as you got there, you sat down on the job. Pulled up an armchair and put up your feet. Got comfortable. A bit complacent. You may be itching to go somewhere else, but what if God already has you exactly where He wants you during this time in your life? Perhaps God's message to you is, "Stay put but *get going*!" Sometimes it's not our circumstances that need to change—it's *us* who need changing.

Because let's remember: we already have an inspiring call from

God! Already and always. His call always rings true and is always challenging, no matter our circumstances.

God's basic call is the same for every Christian. God's basic call is the same at home and abroad, no matter where we live or how we are gifted:

We are called to love the Lord our God with all our heart, soul, mind, and strength (Luke 10:27).

We are called to love our neighbor as ourselves (Luke 10:27).

We are called to love as Christ loved us (John 13:34).

We are called to be a city set on a hill, the light of the world, the salt of the earth (Matthew 5:13–16).

And all of those callings we can answer—we can fulfill—wherever we are right now:

In a classroom fighting narcoleptic attacks in boring classes.

In a dead-end job we don't enjoy.

In a family situation that's not ideal.

In a town we'd love to escape.

In a church full of imperfect people.

Jesus calls us to serve where we are, with what we already have, and with our whole heart—even if we aren't crazy about our current situation or responsibility. When we do, perhaps one day we will be entrusted with more (Matthew 25:14–30). Jesus calls us to give our best and give it now, right where we are.

When Trees Fall

Blue sky, no clouds, spring breeze—a perfect day for yard work, a "heavens declare the glory of God" kind of day. Donnie hums a hymn as he drags a saw across the trunk of a sixty-foot-tall oak tree in his front yard, working alongside his neighbor Todd. Donnie is happy and healthy. Life is good and so is God. Donnie ticks through plans in his mind. So many things he's going to do—take his wife on dates, play with his two young kids, volunteer at church. It will be a full season—go, go, go—but Donnie doesn't mind. He adores his family, enjoys his work, loves serving the Lord.

"Donnie! The transformers!" Donnie looks up, the hum caught in his throat. Todd is gesturing frantically. The tree is falling too soon, angling the wrong way—toward the large green utility boxes in Donnie's yard.

"They'll explode!" Donnie drops his saw. His body reacts without his consent. He leaps forward and shoves the trunk as hard as he can, hoping to redirect its fall—for a moment the tree seems to hang suspended, drifting down in slow motion—and then it shifts, but it shifts the wrong way. And suddenly everything hits hyperdrive. The tree plummets to earth—away from the transformers, but straight toward Donnie.

Donnie wakes in a hospital bed. Memories—and pain—bob slowly to the surface. Familiar faces swim into focus: his wife, Karma; a lifelong family friend, Barbara. "Do I still have feet? And legs?" Donnie rasps through a dry throat and cracked lips.

"Yes," says Karma, placing a straw between his lips.

"Barely," says Barbara with a sardonic smile. "What were you thinking, playing Superman like that?"

Donnie mumbles around the straw.

"In all my years as a trauma ward nurse, I never saw anything this bad," Barbara says, blunt as ever. "That right leg has one of the nastiest breaks ever seen outside a war zone. And your left foot—it's not broken; it's crushed. Congratulations, Donnie. You set records."

Donnie tries to laugh, but even laughter causes catastrophic pain.

Karma hands him the morphine pump.

"So I'm not"—he stumbles over the word—"paralyzed?"

Karma chooses words carefully. "You're not paralyzed, but—there's no guarantee you'll walk again. They're saying recovery will take months." She leans in to kiss his forehead.

"I *will* walk again. I have to." Donnie lays his head back and shuts his eyes. *Well, Lord,* he thinks, *so much for go, go, go.* He is thankful to be alive, determined to hope, but overwhelmed.

"I have a proposal," Barbara says, coming to stand at the foot of the bed. "You need full-time care and major rehab if you want to walk again, and it needs to start *today*. So as long as you're in recovery and I'm not working full-time, I'm coming over to help. I'll be at your house all day every day till you're back on your feet. You know, literally back on your feet. We'll get you walking again even if it kills us both."

Donnie blinks, staggered. He exchanges an unsure glance with Karma. "Barbara, that's so kind of you, but—it's too much. We can't let you do this."

Barbara crosses her arms. "Donnie, you know you cannot talk me out of something once I've made up my daggum mind." (Only she doesn't say *daggum*.) "Besides, if you haven't noticed, your body is a train wreck. If you want to run around in the yard with those kids of yours again, you daggum better let me help you." (Only she still doesn't say *daggum*.) She taps one toe fast against the linoleum and makes the I-dare-you-to-cross-me face Donnie learned *not* to cross when he was about three years old.

It is Karma who speaks. "Barbara, this is just. . . Thank you. We could never repay you."

Barbara shrugs off the thanks and bustles around the room. But as she comes at Donnie waving a fresh IV bag and new bandages, he has a thought. A ridiculous thought. *Maybe there is a way I can repay Barbara after all.* He pictures the "Impossible Prayer List" his church updates every January: at the top of the list of "impossible prayers," scrawled in his mother's best friend's spidery handwriting are the words, "For my daughter Barbara to find faith again and come back to God." Donnie almost smiles to himself. *With God all things are possible. . . .*

Donnie's first morning at home, Barbara shows up as promised. "Let's get down to business, you old tree hugger. From now on, consider me your personal instrument of torture—we're going to take laps around this house every day until those useless legs remember how to walk."

"Okay," Donnie says, "but first. . .can you help me have my morning devotion time? Maybe read aloud to me from the book of Mark? I need to conserve my energy for screaming in pain." He flashes his most innocent smile.

Barbara skewers him with a squinty-eyed look. "Don't you go trying to convert me, Donnie. You know I haven't done church since my twenties. God is your thing and my mother's thing—not mine."

Donnie holds his hands up. "Now what makes you think I would ever try converting a stubborn sinner like you?"

"Stubborn sinner and proud of it," Barbara says, reaching for the Bible. "I'll read to you, you lazy bum, but this is for you, not for me."

"Of course," Donnie says, leaning back against his pillows. "Just start at chapter 1, please."

Barbara opens to the book of Mark: "The beginning of the good news about Jesus the Messiah. . ."

∽

You can probably guess where this story is going. But here's the part you'll never guess. Here's where Donnie and Barbara's story, quietly unfolding in a small house in South Georgia, intersects with mine—in an apartment in downtown Atlanta.

A few months later the phone rings and my husband, Kevin, picks up. "Hey, Dad!" He falls silent for a little too long. "Wait, what? *What* happened?"

I glance up, concerned at his tone.

What's going on? I mouth. Kevin shakes his head, still listening. I scrutinize his expression for clues, but all I can identify on his face is shock. I try to resist my old nemesis, Worst-Case Scenario Disorder, but already my mind is launching a rapid-fire onslaught of awful theories—*the cancer is back, there's been an accident, someone has died.*

"She *what*? Oh my gosh. Both legs?" Kevin is on his feet now, shouting into the phone. "A pine tree? OH! MY! GOSH!"

I knew it. Someone has died, and horribly. Death by tree. "What's happening?" I whimper. Kevin shakes his head. *It's too awful for words,* I think. I'm half crying already, tears teetering on the edge of my eyelids.

But then Kevin is giggling, falling back into a chair with a goofy grin.

My tears freeze in my eyeballs, confused. *Wait, what? Is this good shock?* Frustrated, I lunge for the phone. "Tell me what's going on, you big meanie!"

"Hang on, Dad," Kevin says. He covers the phone with one hand. "It's Aunt Babs," he says, and starts laughing, so hard he's bent in half, barely choking out the words. "She's back."

I shoot him a sideways squint. "From. . .the dead? Because a tree killed her?"

Now Kevin squints at me. "What? No. She's back at church. Back with God. She's *back.*"

I slit my eyes at him even more. "Wait. Are we talking about the same Babs? Your aunt who hasn't set foot in church in two decades and doesn't have a lick of faith? Your aunt who parties like it's 1969?"

"Same Babs. Well—same Babs, totally different. Or so Dad says." Kevin points at the phone. "And get this—her ex-husband Jimbo is getting right with God too."

Now I'm the one stumbling back, collapsing into a chair.

"You'll never believe the story," Kevin says. "It all starts with a falling tree, a pair of broken legs, and a guy named Donnie."

∽

It's been ten years. On the outside very little has changed in Babs's life, but on the inside everything is different. She still lives in the same town, in the same house. She bakes all night at the Dunkin' Donuts down the street; she spends her work breaks racing home to check on her ninety-seven-year-old mother; in the morning she grabs a few hours' sleep, wakes up, reads her Bible, and uses her old nursing skills to care for her mother. She keeps goody bags in her car to give to hungry people she passes on the street. On Saturdays, she hosts a Bible study for the needy at a local laundromat while they wash their clothes for free—"Suds and Souls," she calls it. And every Sunday, Babs is there at church with Donnie and Karma and Jimbo, hands—and heart—lifted to heaven.

This is one of the greatest miracles I have ever had the privilege of witnessing. I took a little creative license filling in some of the dialogue, because time has passed and word-for-word recall is tough, but this story is absolutely true. Donnie is real. The Oak Tree Incident is (unfortunately) real. Aunt Babs is real—and so is her faith.

God used a crippling event in Donnie's life to change Barbara's. God told Donnie to go on a soul-saving mission, but Donnie never left his hometown, his home, or—for a few weeks—even his bed! Donnie could have allowed crushed legs to crush his faith and his spirit, but instead Donnie used those painful months—and the pain itself—to minister to a friend in need.

I pray Donnie's story encourages you if you feel trapped in life—particularly if you suffer illness and physical limitations. You may feel imprisoned in your own home, entombed in your own body, but hear this: God can still use you right where you are. God can still use you *just as you are*, even crippled and crushed and full of pain. Even broken and needy. God still has places He wants you to go, great uses for your life—even meaningful purposes for your pain.

When God Needs Us to Be Still

We often think of the apostle Paul as the most well-traveled missionary of all time, a man constantly on the road and on the go for God. And yet Paul spent several long, lonely stints in prison. My preacher father has often joked that God needed Paul to write most of the New Testament, but the only way He could get Paul to slow down enough to write was by locking him in prison!

Sometimes even when we are healthy physically, we still feel trapped: In a job we hate. A financial bind. A difficult relationship. Are you stuck in life, caught in a situation you never would have chosen for yourself?

If you feel stuck, if God has called you to stay—perhaps your efforts to leave a certain situation have been blocked—I pray you can seek purpose right where you are, for as long as you stay there. Look around for ways to serve. For ways you can minister to others, even if you need some ministering yourself. Who knows what God may have in mind for this time in your life?

When the Grass Is Green Right Where You Are

It's easy to have a "grass is greener" perspective on our Christian life. We hear about other churches and a little voice whispers, *That church sounds so much better than mine. Everybody is so close. They all love—and like!—each other. I bet no one ever gets left out. What's wrong with my church?* Or we hear another minister speak and we think, *That minister sounds so much wiser and more compassionate than mine. Not to mention funnier. If I was in that ministry, I would never get bored and I'd never stop growing. What's wrong with my minister?*

And it's not just churches and preachers. It's everything: The needy elsewhere seem needier. The lost elsewhere seem more lost (and more open to the Gospel). Our hometown, our school, our job, our *life*—it all pales in comparison to everything else, everywhere else. We feel like we have to *go* in order for our lives to count. In order for God to use us. In order to be happy.

And then we face the pesky temptation to compare our own role with others'. When we hear about other believers—how they serve, where they go, what they sacrifice—their Christian lives sound more exciting, more noble, more valuable than our own small life. (This is especially true when we only see others' lives through the filtered, incomplete lens of social media.) *Other Christians matter to God and are useful to God. . .but me? Not so much.* Our own life and service seem small. Unproductive. Uninspiring. And not only does this kind of thinking discourage us, it can also become an excuse for growing spiritually stagnant.

We tell ourselves things like this:

- *My circumstances are the problem.*
- *If I lived in such-and-such a place, I would be on fire for God.*
- *If I had such-and-such a job, I would be motivated.*
- *If I was in such-and-such a role, I would give whole-heartedly.*

I used to think that if I ever went on a mission team to start a new church, I would be the most evangelistic person in the city. Well, you know what? God called me to serve on a mission team, and although I love sharing my faith, evangelism is still a challenge. It's still scary. I am still tempted to be selfish. I still stay quiet sometimes when I should speak up.

As my dad likes to say, "Wherever you go. . .there you are!" A new city won't automatically change us. A job change won't change us. A new relationship won't change us. Change happens in only one place, a place we carry with us everywhere: change happens in our hearts. No matter where we live or what our role may be, we can change, we can grow, and we can bravely give ourselves to God.

Everyday Christianity

How many times do we unintentionally overlook opportunities for serving Christ in our daily lives? We miss them because we see them all the time. Our eyes—and hearts—skip past familiar needs, old heartaches, because familiarity has bred blindness. Dullness. Life gets busy, our schedule gets tight, and we accidentally walk past lonely neighbors needing friends. Classmates struggling with depression. Recent divorcees longing for a listening ear. New parents needing a hot meal or a kind word. Colossians 4 urges us,

"Devote yourselves to prayer, being watchful and thankful. . . . Be wise in the way you act towards outsiders; make the most of every opportunity" (verses 2, 5). Jesus often lamented dullness, saying, "Do you have eyes but fail to see, and ears but fail to hear?" (Mark 8:18). Let us pray to see and hear the needs around us.

I have always loved this small description from Acts 5:42: "Day after day, in the temple courts and from house to house, they never stopped teaching and proclaiming the good news that Jesus is the Messiah."

The apostles shared Christ in the temple, but also from house to house. It's not automatically better to serve *out there* or *over there*. It's not less godly—or even less brave—to share your faith with a neighbor two doors down than a stranger a world away. It's not more righteous to serve an orphan across the ocean than a foster child across town. All children need love; all these callings— missions near and far—are godly endeavors.

My grandparents, Frank and Jane Guba, became Christians in their thirties, when a preacher came to their South Florida home and taught them the Bible. After their baptism, they served God together from that same house for more than forty years; my grandmother went home to Jesus there, and my grandfather still lives there now.

At age sixty-five they retired and began looking for ways to give in their free time. South Florida is filled with nursing homes. While some are vibrant, active communities, others are sad, sterile facilities filled with lonely seniors. Some receive no visitors—perhaps they have no family; maybe they have outlived all their friends. My grandparents decided that these people would be their ministry. Several times a week, they went room to room in senior homes, making friends and leading Bible studies. For two decades they offered friendship, brought laughter, shone light. Over the years they brought many seniors to the Lord. Most of those "baby Christians" were too, well, old to ever attend church. But my grandparents brought church, and salvation, to them. Quietly, without fanfare or thanks, Frank and Jane Guba did great things for God right there in their hometown. They stayed home, but how far they went!

Remember the beer-drinking, rugby-playing girl I mentioned in chapter 1? The one I wanted to share the Gospel with even though she intimidated me? I chased her down across campus and introduced myself, saying, "Hey, I really appreciated what you said in class about hypocrisy in Christianity. I totally agree with you, and I'd love to talk more about it." And from there—that one simple conversation—Cat and I struck up a friendship. She soon told me that two nights before we met, she sat outside on a fraternity bench, smoking. As she smoked she prayed her heart out, pleading, "God, if you are real, please send me a friend to lead me to You." For the next eight months, Cat and I met in the student union with Bibles and bagels—and at the end of it, Cat found the true faith she'd been looking for. Turns out true Christianity had been right there in her Bible all along. Today, twenty years later, Cat still lives a short drive from the university, still volunteers there often, and wherever she goes—on campus or around town—Cat still shares the faith she found.

⟳

Legion wanted to go somewhere new. He dreamed of spending his days traveling with Jesus, but that wasn't Jesus' plan. Perhaps Jesus knew that no one could be more effective in the Decapolis than Legion. Was Legion already a local legend? The star of horror stories told around Decapolis campfires—the haunted man who haunted the tombs? If so, imagine the shock, the amazement, the praise that would have rippled across those towns as Legion returned home carrying his tale of redemption.

As with Legion, God may be calling you to stay home—but staying home doesn't mean staying the same. Even if Jesus is calling you to stay, He is still calling you to move forward: Go deep. Love hard. Grow strong. . .right where you are.

Let's Go Deeper. . .

For Further Study
Read Acts 9:32–43 (Aeneas and Dorcas) and Acts 10 (Cornelius). Like Legion, these people served God in great ways from their own hometowns.

Journal Prompt
1. If God is calling you to stay where you are, how might He want you to "get going"?
2. Where has the "spiritual grass" seemed greener to you—another city? A different role? A different job? How can you find contentment and purpose where you are?
3. Have you noticed any needs close to home that you could meet?

Prayer Prompt
While we live in these earthly bodies, we groan and sigh, but it's not that we want to die and get rid of these bodies that clothe us. Rather, we want to put on our new bodies so that these dying bodies will be swallowed up by life. God himself has prepared us for this, and as a guarantee he has given us his Holy Spirit.

So we are always confident, even though we know that as long as we live in these bodies we are not at home with the Lord. For we live by believing and not by seeing. Yes, we are fully confident, and we would rather be away from these earthly bodies, for then we will be at home with the Lord. So whether we are here in this body or away from this body, our goal is to please him. . . .

Because we understand our fearful responsibility to the Lord, we work hard to persuade others. God knows we are sincere, and I hope you know this, too.
2 Corinthians 5:4–9, 11 NLT

11
When God Calls without Warning

Abigail's Story

Based on 1 Samuel 25

$\mathcal{A}$bigail stands in the center of the storeroom as activity swirls around her. A torrent of servants floods in and out, carrying sacks and jugs.

"No, not there!" Abigail says to a young servant girl placing a jug on the wrong shelf. "That goes over there."

"Yes, ma'am; sorry, ma'am." Red-faced, the girl scuttles out, ducking to avoid the disapproving glare of a weathered senior servant standing in the doorway.

"Apologies, my lady," says the wrinkled woman. "That one doesn't know her right hand from her left."

Abigail smiles. "It's fine. If that's the worst thing that happens today, I count it a blessing."

A teenage boy skids through the doorway, panting. "Nabal says we need more wine for the feast. A lot more wine."

"Come here, Joel," Abigail says. She places a hand under his chin and tilts his face up. His cheek is red—too red.

"Who hit you?" she whispers, so the others cannot hear.

Joel drops his eyes. Abigail pulls him through the throng of rushing people, into a corner with sacks of grain stacked high.

"Was it my husband?" she asks quietly. Joel blinks at the ground and shrugs.

She sets her shoulders. "If Nabal thinks there is not enough wine, that is not your fault." She pauses a beat too long, tempted to say, *"It's Nabal's"*—instead she pushes out the words, "It's mine."

Joel licks his lips and says, "He said I have to go and report back to him right away, or—or—" He says nothing, but his hands make fists and his breaths come fast. Fear fills his eyes. In her mind's eye, Abigail hears the whistle of Nabal's whip, the thud of his fists, the muffled cries of his victims. Sounds she has heard too many times over the long years as his wife.

Fighting a surge of anger, Abigail places a hand on the boy's shoulder. "The distribution of goods is my responsibility. I will report back to Nabal myself," she says. "You go help out in the fields with the shearing. Stay out there. If you don't show your face to Nabal for a few days, I promise he'll forget all about it."

Joel looks up at her with a hint of hope sparking in his eyes. "Really?"

Abigail gives his shoulder a squeeze. "Really. Nabal may have a fast temper, but he has a short memory." *Especially once he starts drinking tonight.*

A smile flickers across Joel's face. "Thank you, my lady."

She gives him a gentle nudge toward the door. "Now go. Find some sheep to shear."

She watches his back dart for the door. The acid of anger tries to worm its way up her gut, but she breathes deep to tamp it down.

"But Mother, what do I do if he's—cruel?" Her own tear-strained voice, the night before her wedding. "I've heard rumors."

Her mother's face, lined with wisdom, her eyes dark with sadness. She lays a warm hand on Abigail's cheek, and Abigail leans into it, pressing her own hand atop her mother's, memorizing its feel, wondering if Nabal will ever let her see her family again after they are wed. "You must find ways around his cruelty," her mother says. "Rumor has it your betrothed is wealthy but unwise—not for nothing do people call him Nabal, 'the Fool.'" A smile plays at her mouth. "I did not raise a stupid daughter. I raised you to be strong and smart and to think for yourself. Abigail, darling, you are clever, and in time you will find ways to. . .work around him. You must not be disrespectful or rebellious—that would be the ultimate folly—but if you think hard and pray harder, you can play to his pride and just. . .work around him. What do you think I myself have done with your father all these years?" She drops a wink, and Abigail bites back a laugh of surprise. She has never once heard her mother speak ill of her father—not even when Abigail has tried to draw it out of her.

But now she thinks: Mother comforting bruised servants after Father has gone to bed. Mother hustling Abigail from the room when Father's temper flares. Mother rising before dawn to pray in peace before the household wakes and Father calls for wine. Mother's smile, the sun that has always brightened their home when it could have been—should have been—a place of darkness.

Her mother draws her into a hug. "I could not talk your father out of arranging this marriage for you."

"Why not?" Abigail chokes out the words, fighting the burn in her eyes.

"It was too good an alliance to pass up." Her mother's voice is tight, laced with a bitterness Abigail has never heard there before. Her mother clears her throat, and her voice is even, careful. "The Lord will see you through, my daughter. He will watch over you. He will be there to protect you even when I am not. You must be strong, and you must be smart. You can do this."

Abigail sags into the hug. The Lord will watch over me. I can do this.

Shaking her head to dispel the memory, Abigail steps back into the bustle of people. She grabs her abandoned list from the nearest shelf and begins rattling off orders. As hours pass, the room grows hot. Abigail's dress sticks to her back, and her hair plasters to the back of her neck.

An hour later, there's a commotion in the doorway, servants shouting, "Hey!" as a voice insists, "Let me through! I have a message!"

The crowd parts and Joel skids to a stop in front of Abigail, white-faced.

"Joel! Are you hurt?"

He shakes his head, breathing so hard he cannot speak.

"Everyone back to work!" she says, and with a lot of mumbling and curious backward glances, the crowd resumes its activity.

She places a hand on Joel's arm and pulls him back to the quiet corner. "What is it?"

"It's—it's David, my lady."

She squints her eyes at him, searching her memory for the name. "David? We have no one in our household named Da–"

"David the giant killer. The warrior. The man on the run from King Saul."

Abigail's eyes widen. "Oh, that David." She tilts her head sideways. "I'm sorry, what does David have to do with us?"

Joel rattles words so fast she can hardly follow: "David and his men have been staying near our shepherds for several weeks. He sent messengers from the wilderness to greet our master—they only wanted some food as thanks—but Nabal insulted them."

Abigail's stomach turns to stone.

"David and his men were very good to our shepherds. Night and day they were a wall around us—they kept our men and our sheep safe from beasts and thieves." Joel stops to suck in a quick breath. "David's men were furious. They rode away fast, but they're coming back. David will not—he cannot—allow his name to be so insulted."

Icy sweat trickles down Abigail's back. "This is bad," she whispers. "This is very bad."

Joel places a hand on his bruising cheek. "Please, my lady, David has hundreds of men. Please talk to our master before it's too late."

Abigail paces between shelves, thoughts racing. "I dare not speak to Nabal about this."

"But my lady—" Joel's voice cracks. "They're coming back to kill us all."

"I *know*," Abigail says, a little more sharply than she intends.

She looks up at Joel and softens her voice with an effort. "I'm thinking."

Her mother's voice echoes: *"Be strong. Be smart. Work around him."*

With a deep breath, Abigail claps her hands and steps into the middle of the room. "Attention, everyone! Eyes on me!"

People slow their movements, whispering in confusion.

"David the giant slayer and mighty warrior is headed here with hundreds of men. If you do not do exactly as I say, you will not survive the night. Am I understood?" The room stills, silenced beneath a blanket of fear.

Heads nod.

"I need twenty of you to stay with Adina, carrying on preparations for the feast." She leans in to speak quietly to Adina. "Nabal must see you working, and you must appear to be doing the work of forty people; do you understand? He must not suspect that work has slowed or that any servants are otherwise occupied."

"Yes, ma'am. We will do the work"—Adina half smiles—"and make the noise—of forty people. Our master will be fully distracted."

Abigail flashes a quick smile and squeezes the old woman's arm. "Thank you."

"The rest of you, we have a lot of work to do, and fast. Come close and listen. I have a plan."

She rattles off instructions, a commander sending troops in every direction.

"Now what are you waiting for? Say your prayers, and let's get going."

∽

For many years, Abigail wakes each morning to a somewhat predictable life. Every day she manages her household. Finds ways to work around her foolish husband with his drinking problem and sour disposition. Fights to have faith, to believe that God is with her. . .

Until the day everything goes sideways. The day a terrified

servant comes sprinting back with the news, "David and a small army of angry men are headed this way, and if you don't do something about it, we're all going to die!"

Abigail has to move—and fast. The Bible tells us, "Abigail acted quickly" (1 Samuel 25:18). She swings into action, packing up meals to (literally) feed an army, a peace offering she hopes will not come too late. She herself leads the caravan carrying the food. When she reaches David and his men, Abigail throws herself to the ground in front of their swords, begging for mercy. Her speech is clever, eloquent, endearing. She is both humble and forthright, challenging David's temper even as she appeases his ego.

With no warning and little time to prepare, Abigail faces the most dangerous moment of her life, and she shines. She eases David's temper, soothes his pride, and averts catastrophe.

David says, "Praise be to the LORD, the God of Israel, who has sent you today to meet me. May you be blessed for your good judgment and for keeping me from bloodshed this day and from avenging myself with my own hands. . . . Go home in peace. I have heard your words and granted your request" (1 Samuel 25:32–33, 35).

Not only does Abigail's action prevent the future king from making a huge mistake, but she also saves many lives. When Nabal sobers up and hears what happened, his heart fails. Within ten days, he is dead.

And the story isn't over yet—check out what happens next:

> Then David sent word to Abigail, asking her to become his wife. His servants went to Carmel and said to Abigail, "David has sent us to you to take you to become his wife."
>
> She bowed down with her face to the ground and said, "I am your servant and am ready to serve you and wash the feet of my lord's servants."
>
> 1 SAMUEL 25:39–41

How's that for a crazy twist and a fairy-tale ending? David gets justice and Abigail gets to become (eventually) a queen.

When You Feel Stuck. . .Keep Growing

When Abigail married Nabal, she had no idea her life would one day take a dramatic twist. As far as this "intelligent and beautiful woman" knew, thanks to the culture of her day, she must remain married to a "surly and mean" man for the rest of her life (1 Samuel 25:3).[1]

How easy it would have been for Abigail to give in to bitterness! To spend her life hating Nabal and feeling sorry for herself. To dig in her heels and refuse to be happy in this life that, chances are, considering the customs of her time, her father had chosen for her.

But when Abigail whirls into action and delivers her speech, we see the fruit of her faith and growth through hardship. We see a woman who has not wasted her suffering. All those months and years learning to work with and around a difficult husband have prepared her for this, the most dangerous conversation of her life. All those years fighting for faith, learning self-control and discretion, she had no idea God was getting her ready to save lives and become a queen. . .but when the time came, Abigail was ready.

Ready, Set. . .

Jesus spoke often of the need to get ourselves ready, the need to be prepared—prepared for the unexpected and, most importantly, prepared for God's coming. Many of His stories circled around the theme of readiness: the parable of the rich fool (Luke 12:13–21); the parable of the talents (Matthew 25:14–30); the parable of the ten virgins (Matthew 25:1–13).

> *"Be on guard! Be alert! You do not know when that time will come. It's like a man going away: He leaves his house and puts his servants in charge, each with*

*their assigned task, and tells the one at the door to
keep watch.*

*"Therefore keep watch because you do not know
when the owner of the house will come back—
whether in the evening, or at midnight, or when the
rooster crows, or at dawn. If he comes suddenly, do
not let him find you sleeping. What I say to you, I say
to everyone: 'Watch!'"*

MARK 13:33–37

Some of you reading this are already in the throes of transition.
Jesus has said, "Go," and you're sprinting like mad, desperate to
keep up. Scrambling to find the courage, confidence, and cool head
you need to match His blistering pace.

Others aren't in a time of transition (yet)—you are enjoying a season of peace and calm. Perhaps you picked up this book
because life feels stagnant and you yearn for excitement, for spiritual adventure. Don't worry. . .if life in Christ seems boring right
now, it rarely stays that way for long!

Jesus calls us to use times of peace as times of preparation.
In-between times can be in-process times, opportunities to:

- Practice spiritual disciplines that anchor our faith and
  deepen our convictions.
- Read and memorize scripture so that when Satan
  attacks, we are armed with an arsenal of scriptures
  (Luke 4:1–13; Ephesians 6:13–17).
- Fill our faith tank full for days when difficulties drain it.
- Form strong spiritual relationships to see us through
  painful times.
- Build a prayer life—an intimacy with God—that can
  weather tough storms.

In his letter to the Ephesians, Paul urges us, "Put on the full armor of God, so that when the day of evil comes, you may be able to stand your ground, and after you have done everything, to stand" (Ephesians 6:13).

When It's Time to Clean House

We've covered some deep topics in this book. Honestly? Writing this book has been an intensely emotional process for me. It has made me dig deep and face demons. Fear demons, emotional demons, I-am-prideful-and-I-don't-always-like-God's-plan demons.

Several months ago I got into Deep-Clean-Every-Nook-and-Cranny-in-the-House Mode. When I get into this mode, my family has learned to hide. (Because if I find you sitting there on your lazy behind watching TV, I will give you a job to do, and it will take hours.) So in a strangely quiet house, I put the hose attachment onto the vacuum and started attacking baseboards: Elizabeth versus Cole Fur, Round 7,436. We adore our old Labrador retriever, Cole, but his black fur is my archenemy. It's a losing battle—a disgusting battle—and yet I fight on.

Down on my hands and knees, I started vacuum-crawling my way around the kitchen. I was working up a sweat, but it was strangely satisfying work, knowing I was cleaning the nookiest nooks and the cranniest crannies, watching the furry baseboards regain their pure white glow. In a hard-to-reach corner behind a chair, poking around with the hose extension, I felt something move. Ducking my head down to peer underneath the chair, I saw something small, round, and brown hiding in the dark. *What in the world?* Using the end of the hose, I nudged the brown thing out from under the chair—out rolled a piece of chocolate! And not just a regular old piece of chocolate, either—this was a fancy piece left over from the kids' Valentine's Day boxes. How in the world it had escaped I didn't want to know, but I had a little chuckle, observed a moment of silence for the waste of a precious piece of expensive chocolate, threw it into the trash, and kept working.

I determinedly continued vacuum-crawling my way around

the house—through the living room, around the fireplace, into the kids' playroom. In another hard-to-reach corner, I spotted something else hiding in shadow. Something small, round, and brown. *What's going on here? Did Kevin and the kids have a secret chocolate fight last Valentine's Day?* Again I dug around with the hose attachment, nudging the brown thing out of darkness, into the light. . .only this time, it wasn't chocolate that came rolling out. It was a piece of fossilized dog poop.

I was too shocked even to scream. I just sat there, rocking back on my heels, gasping for breath, fighting the urge to vomit. I cannot adequately describe the horror. If there is such a thing as PTPFD—Post-Traumatic Poop-Finding Disorder—I am sure I acquired it in that awful moment. (I pray I have not unwittingly passed it on to you. I hereby interrupt this paragraph for those of you who need a gag-into-a-bag break. I know. This is revolting, and I am sorry. I promise we're done with the super-gross stuff now.)

You'd better believe there was some frenzied bleaching going on for the next ten minutes—the floor, the vacuum, my hands. (Don't judge the bleach, my friends—I'm sorry, but if you find fossilized poop in a corner of your kids' playroom, you just have to say, "Bring on the bleach.") When I finally stopped gagging, I figured out what had happened: Cole had recently had an accident in the house, and somehow this one little gem had rolled away into a dark corner, unseen. We thought we had thoroughly cleaned, but we had missed something.

I promise, I have a spiritual point in all of this! I uncovered more than just chocolate and poop in my house that day; I also discovered the weirdest life lesson I've ever learned: When you start deep-cleaning, you never know what you're going to find. Maybe a little chocolate, maybe a little poop. This holds true not just for houses, but also for hearts. The closer we look and the deeper we clean, the more hidden things we find. In some corners we'll find beauty and joy—strengths of character we never realized we had, gifts from God we've never appreciated—*Oh yay, chocolate!* And yes, in other corners we'll find sins we have overlooked, resentments we didn't realize we were holding on to—*Oh gross, poop!*

In the pages of this book I imagine you have confronted some of your own hidden corners. In some corners you have probably found some things you wish you hadn't: weak faith, ugly fears, festering wounds. From one weak and wounded soul to another, I say, *Don't give up!* Get out the bleach, clean up the mess, and keep moving forward. Because what's the alternative—kick it back into the corner, pray no one else notices it, and hope it just magically disappears on its own? Um, no. When we find gross things in our houses—or our hearts—we have to deal with them. We have to clean them up.

But I pray your "deep clean" has also surprised you with hidden joys: previously undiscovered gifts, greater courage, fresh growth. Perhaps, like Abigail, you have realized you are stronger than you thought. Wiser than you knew. Maybe you have seen the grace of Jesus in a new light, a more personal light, a Mary-alone-with-Jesus-in-the-sunrise light. Maybe you have felt the arms of your heavenly Father reaching out to hug you, heard His happy voice whisper, "I'm so proud of you!"

When God Calls Us Home

We don't know when God is going to call. He seems to enjoy surprises. But like Abigail, we all need to use what time we have to get ready.

Usually when God says, "Go," He's calling us to move, to give, and to grow in some new way. And we each get our own calls—our own lives, our own burdens, our own blessings. Our own unique ways of walking with Him and serving Him.

But there is one call we all get in the end. Eventually God is going to call and say, "It's time to go home. Time to *come* home. Home to heaven with Me." And that's the call we need to prepare for more than any other.

Near the end of Paul's life, he wrote to Timothy, his son in the faith:

> *For I am already on the point of being sacrificed; the time of my departure has come. I have fought the good fight, I have finished the race, I have kept the faith. Henceforth there is laid up for me the crown of righteousness, which the Lord, the righteous judge, will award to me on that Day, and not only to me but also to all who have loved his appearing.*
>
> 2 TIMOTHY 4:6–8 RSV

I have fought the good fight.
I have finished the race.

How I long to be able to say those words at the end of my life—that I have given God my all. Fought well. Finished strong.

Isn't that the way we all want to go? Giving everything we have to God for as many days as He grants? Not wasting our life hampered by fear, regret, guilt, or selfishness?

Let's get ready. Like Abigail, let's use in-between times in useful ways, preparing ourselves—cleaning house, cleaning hearts—so that when God says, "It's time," we can stand up and say, "I'm ready to go."

Let's Go Deeper. . .

For Further Study
Read Abigail's entire speech in 1 Samuel 25. Notice how she appeals to David's pride but also speaks the truth. Masterful!

Journal Prompt
1. Consider the current difficulties in your life. What character traits might God be allowing you to develop that could serve

His greater purposes later?

2. What one spiritual discipline could you focus on right now (prayer, Bible study, scripture memory, relationships, openness) to help prepare you for future spiritual challenges?

3. What chocolate have you uncovered in your heart recently? What, uh, gross stuff have you discovered?

Prayer Prompt

When you lie down, you will not be afraid;
*   when you lie down, your sleep will be sweet.*
Have no fear of sudden disaster
*   or of the ruin that overtakes the wicked,*
for the LORD will be at your side
*   and will keep your foot from being snared.*
PROVERBS 3:24–26

12
When Your Time Has Come

Peter's Story, Part 2

Based on Luke 22:47–62 and Matthew 26:47–75

He can't get warm. He's been avoiding the fire—the light on his face. Avoiding the small crowd clustered together—warming hands, stamping feet, swapping rumors. Rumors about Jesus.

But the cold is making Peter's muscles stiff, his fingers useless. Even his bones are cold, rubbing up against each other, creaking. *If they come for you and you're stiff with cold, you won't be able to run.*

He inches closer to the reaching light. Hovers just outside the circle of gossip. Usually he finds firelight comforting, inviting, an old friend—so many fireside talks he has spent with Jesus and the other guys, pondering, bantering, debating—but tonight's fire glows sinister. The flames writhe, thirsty serpents. The embers glow, angry red.

Blood. He looks down at his hands, speckled with the blood of the high priest's servant. His stomach twists at the memory: rage and fear boiling over; the way he lashed out with feral shriek and flashing sword; a bright spray of blood; Malchus's keening scream, hands clutched to the side of his head; Jesus' rebuke, a slap of sound—*"Put that away! All who live by the sword will die by the sword. . . ."*

He picks at the crusted drops on his hands. Scrubs at them with the edge of his cloak. The stain remains.

I have spilled blood.

"This is My blood, poured out for you," the Lord had said

just hours before, holding up a glass. What did He mean? Did He know what was coming? He must have known; He always seemed to know. But surely He didn't mean—surely they wouldn't kill Him?

Feeling eyes on him, Peter looks around. Two men in servants' robes are throwing looks his way, heads bent together. Peter casts an anxious glance toward the high priest's massive house, the windows flickering with candlelight. *I was a fool to come. Malchus works here. Surely he has already returned, given the servants and guards my description.*

A soft tap on his elbow makes him jump. "What?" he barks, fists already up.

A teenaged servant girl stands looking up at him, fire flickering orange in her eyes. He lowers his fists to his waist. Keeps them clenched. He watches her eyes take in his robe—curse his wife for adding the Galilean-style stitching—then travel across the spots of blood. Peter backs up a step. The girl speaks loudly, loud enough for the two men to hear. "This man was with Him. Jesus. The traitor."

"What?" Peter blusters, trying to summon a casual laugh. "I don't know what you're talking about. I'm here to bring a case before Caiaphas in the morning."

The girl narrows her eyes—she is brash enough to look him in the eye. He forces himself to hold her gaze until she blushes and turns away. The two men go back to their conversation. Peter stretches and shrinks into the shadows near the courtyard wall. Hides in the darkness and cold, his body and brain going numb. He cannot think, cannot leave, cannot feel. He finds one line and repeats it over and over: *Jesus will be free soon. Free soon. Free soon.*

An hour later, with his feet turned to frigid blocks, he shuffles in closer to the fire. Tries to warm his feet, bring life to his toes.

A group of male servants emerges from the shadows, jostling Peter as they take places by the fire. Peter coughs at the heavy scent of manure clinging to their clothes. "The inside girls said He won't say anything in His own defense," says one.

Peter doesn't move, caught between wanting to hear more and wanting to get away. But if he runs now, they'll know. *I have spilled blood. They will come for me next.*

"Stupid Nazarenes," snorts another, an old man with a voice like gravel. "Worthless idiots."

Peter barks an attempt at a laugh, trying to blend in.

They turn eyes on him. "You heard about this man?" says a teenager with mottled skin. "The one who calls himself the king?"

Peter shrugs, head down, hands to the flames. He hopes they don't see his fingers trembling.

The old man leans in closer. "Where you from anyway?"

"Here and there," Peter grunts. "Fisherman."

"Fisherman!" the old man says, the word an accusation.

Peter's eyes jump up to meet the man's face— too late, he tries to wipe the naked fear from his face. "You are one of them!" the man says, wagging a crooked finger. "The Nazarene's disciples!" Two other men take steps forward, wide eyes gleaming red in the firelight.

"I am not! Can't a man come to seek justice from the high priest without being persecuted?" Fear waylays his mind. *Fight, fight*: it's all he can think. Fear mimics rage: the old curses spill, familiar words from an old life.

The old man listens openmouthed. Tongue tasting of bitterness, Peter stands spent, shoulders wide and heaving.

The old man raises his palms. "Calm down. No need to wake the house."

Peter slumps on a stump and hunches into his cloak. Desperate to leave, but trapped by his own words. If he runs, they'll know. *Head down, stay safe.* He rocks for warmth, his mind a careful blank, wiped clean of all thoughts but one: *Head down, stay safe.*

Chatter stays quiet for a while. People drift in and out. Two girls in servants' robes emerge from the house and set down their baskets by the fire.

"What's happening inside? With the prisoner?" A new voice, a male voice, comes from the dancing shadows on the other side of the fire. Peter can't make out a face.

"He still won't talk," says one girl.

"Caiaphas is sending him to"—the second girl yawns—"Pilate."

Peter's insides shrivel, doused in cold water. He speaks without knowing he's going to. "When?"

"First light," drawls the sleepy girl.

"Why do *you* care?" says the voice from the shadows.

All eyes are on Peter.

"I don't," he says, in the dullest voice he can muster. "Just curious."

A darkness detaches from the shadows, taking the shape of a tall man. He saunters around the fire and stands close to Peter. Too close. The man holds his hands toward the flames as his eyes scour Peter's face.

"What are you looking at?" Peter demands. His heartbeat thunders in his ears.

A smile starts across the man's face and stops halfway. "You were with Him," he says. "You're from Galilee, just like Him."

Peter jumps up, fire and ice—heat burning his face, fear freezing his heart. "I am not! What is with you people?" He pushes the man with one hand, and the man rocks back a step. Peter should stop, stomp away, make a dramatic exit, but he can't stop talking, can't stop cursing. All voices hush, all eyes lock on Peter. The only sounds are the fire consuming wood and the curses streaming from Peter's mouth. His voice raises to a full shout. "On the stones of the temple I swear"—between breaths he glances up, sees Jesus framed by the light in the open doorway, but it's too late to dam the flood of words; Peter keeps shouting, his mouth unable to catch up with his eyes—"I never knew the man!" His words ring cold across the courtyard stones.

Jesus looks up. Stares straight at Peter. A moonbeam shines just so, lighting His face, illuminating His expression.

Not angry—hurt. Sad. Alone.

"Before the rooster crows, you will deny Me three times."

"Never, Lord! I am ready to die with You!"

Peter gurgles, choking on shame, and reaches a hand toward Jesus, but He has already turned away. The soldiers prod Him forward and He stumbles—harsh laughter, a thump, a cry of pain—and Jesus is swallowed by the crowd, muscled out through the gates.

The crowd follows the soldiers, enjoying the show.

Peter stands alone. Though he stands by the fire, he has never been colder. Though he stands in the light, he has never been darker.

He runs, tears streaming, chest spasming. His foot hits something and he sprawls, hurtling face-first into dirt. Something warm spreads across his forehead. He feels no pain, just rolls to his side, breathing in dirt, bleeding out hope.

☙

Jesus knew I would fail! He told me I would deny Him! Is this what He wanted? Why call me in the first place if He knew I'd only cower in the end?

We can only imagine the thoughts that must have run through Peter's head in the days following Jesus' death. Three dark days when all seemed lost. Dare he even call himself by the Lord's nickname, Peter (meaning "rock"), anymore? Three times he had denied his beloved friend. For one insane night he had abandoned the new man—Peter the rock, Peter the water-walker, Peter the feisty friend of Jesus—and become his old self again: Simon the fisherman, Simon the weak, Simon the crass.

Have you ever been there? Lost yourself in one cataclysmic spiritual failure—forgotten Jesus, forgotten who you have become, forgotten it all? And then the storm passes, the fear calms, and you're left like Peter, alone outside with your guilt and your tears?

When We Can't See the Plan

I suspect Peter's courtyard denials were not *just* precipitated by fear. Peter and the other eleven disciples had long misunderstood Jesus' ultimate purpose.

Jesus had tried to warn the Twelve, tried to prepare them for what was coming. So many times He had spoken of His future suffering and resurrection. But Luke tells us, "The disciples did not understand any of this. Its meaning was hidden from them, and they did not know what he was talking about" (Luke 18:31–34). In their defense, how could they grasp what was to come—death and then the unthinkable, the impossible, the unimaginable: resurrection? Sometimes God's plans—and His calls—stretch so far beyond human imagination that we can't keep up, can't wrap our limited earthbound perspectives around them.

And sometimes even when understanding starts to dawn—clouded sunrise—still we resist, still we push truth away:

> *From that time on Jesus began to explain to his disciples that he must go to Jerusalem and suffer many things at the hands of the elders, the chief priests and the teachers of the law, and that he must be killed and on the third day be raised to life.*
>
> *Peter took him aside and began to rebuke him. "Never, Lord!" he said. "This shall never happen to you!"*
>
> *Jesus turned and said to Peter, "Get behind me, Satan! You are a stumbling block to me; you do not have in mind the concerns of God, but merely human concerns."*
>
> Matthew 16:21–23

"Never, Lord! This shall never happen to you!"
"Get behind me, Satan!"

What a painful moment for Peter. What an embarrassment. Here he is, trying to defend his friend, thinking he's being noble, but instead of thanking Peter for his loyalty, Jesus rebukes him. And this is no quiet reprimand—Jesus publicly calls him *Satan*. Yikes.

Though Peter's desire to defend and protect the One he loves is admirable, it is misplaced. Peter didn't understand that Jesus had to go to His death. But we find a lesson in Jesus' words: "You don't have in mind the concerns of God, but merely human concerns."

Isn't that the way it goes? We worry about our own safety, comfort, and reputation. Jesus worried about none of those things. He lost Himself completely in the will of God. What God needed, Jesus gave. When God called, Jesus responded. When God needed sacrifice, Jesus said, "Here am I." No matter the pain, no matter the price.

Sometimes God calls us—or someone we love—to make a sacrifice. And to our human minds, it's too much. The cost is too great. It doesn't make sense. *There's too much suffering in that. That plan doesn't have a happy ending. That can't be the will of God.* And although we don't mean to, we stand in the way of God's call *simply because it's difficult.*

Again at the Last Supper, Jesus warns Peter what is coming:

> *"This cup is the new covenant in my blood, which is poured out for you. . . .*
>
> *"Simon, Simon, Satan has asked to sift all of you as wheat. But I have prayed for you, Simon, that your faith may not fail. And when you have turned back, strengthen your brothers."*
>
> *But [Peter] replied, "Lord, I am ready to go with you to prison and to death."*
>
> *Jesus answered, "I tell you, Peter, before the rooster crows today, you will deny three times that you know me."*
>
> LUKE 22:20, 31–34

Peter thinks he is ready, thinks he understands the cost, but when it comes to it, he's not ready at all. Hours later, out in the high priest's cold courtyard, Peter is still fighting the plan. Still refusing to understand, refusing to accept what Jesus has come to do. Still trying to find a way out of the suffering. *They're going to let Jesus go soon. There's no use in me getting arrested too. We just have to make it through the night, make it out alive. He'll be free soon, free soon. . . .*

Peter has forgotten—or perhaps chosen to forget—so many of Jesus' words, the words about courage and crosses, denial and death: *"Take up your cross and follow Me. . . . If you do not carry your own cross, you cannot be My disciple. . . . Whoever wants to save their life will lose it. . . ."*

These are hard words. Not comforting. They don't look pretty even when we dress them up with calligraphy and watercolors.

Obedience. Surrender. Submission. These were the truths Peter fought against not just this awful night in the courtyard, but throughout his time with Jesus.

In fact, Peter is still fighting even after the resurrection. One morning, Peter and the disciples go out fishing, and Jesus appears on the beach. Peter, recognizing his friend even from afar, gets so excited that he throws all his clothes on, dives into the water, and swims to shore.

Dripping wet, he stands before the Lord, out of breath and needing forgiveness. There on the beach Jesus restores Peter, giving him three chances to publicly declare his love and loyalty—for each denial, a do-over; for each betrayal, grace. But then Jesus says this:

> *"Very truly I tell you, when you were younger you dressed yourself and went where you wanted; but when you are old you will stretch out your hands, and someone else will dress you and lead you where you do not want to go." Jesus said this to indicate the kind of*

death by which Peter would glorify God. Then he said
to him, "Follow me!"

JOHN 21:18–19

"Someone else will dress you and lead you where you do not want to go." Those are sobering words. Scary words. Words prophesying Peter's martyrdom, the final cost of his discipleship. But poor Peter, he is still fighting—here is his response:

> Peter turned and saw that the disciple whom Jesus
> loved was following them. (This was the one who
> had leaned back against Jesus at the supper and had
> said, "Lord, who is going to betray you?") When Peter
> saw him, he asked, "Lord, what about him?"
> Jesus answered, "If I want him to remain alive
> until I return, what is that to you? You must follow me."

JOHN 21:20–22

Oh, Peter. This is why we love him, why we relate to him. He's so often pushing back against the plan. Saying exactly what he thinks. Giving us a little break in the emotional tension. Here after an intense moment of reconciliation with Jesus, in what should be a profound and meaningful moment, Peter hijacks the conversation and the mood.

Not only does Peter resist the plan, he also resents his own role when he compares it with someone else's (traditionally the "disciple whom Jesus loved" is identified as John). We can almost hear the thoughts churning through Peter's mind: *Wait, that's not fair! I don't want to be the only martyr! If I have to suffer, then so should John. He ran away from Gethsemane too!*

But Jesus says, "What is that to you? You must follow Me."

Sometimes it's tempting to look around and compare our calling—and our burdens—with other Christians':

Why is his life so much easier than mine?

Why didn't I get great parents like she has? If I had a family like hers, I'd be in a totally different place spiritually and emotionally.

Why is money so easy for them? If I'd been born into money like they were, I'd be such a different person. If I didn't have to work so much and always feel stressed about debt and bills, I could serve God better—I could do everything better.

Why did I have to experience all those awful things when I was young? Why can't I have her *childhood instead of mine? If I could have come to God whole and undamaged, I could be so much more effective. I have seen too much to be of any use to God.*

I don't mean to speak lightly of deep wounds or great loss. We each bear different burdens: Some bear the burden of a painful upbringing or an absent parent, others the burden of betrayal by a spouse. Some bear a difficult role in ministry, others persecution and—yes, even today—martyrdom for Christ. Some are single but long to be loved; others are infertile but long for a baby. Some enjoy good health; others endure chronic illness. Some are called to long life; others to early graves.

In our eyes, from our limited perspectives, it's not fair. It doesn't shake out evenly. Psalm 131 has always helped me find peace when I am tempted to try to "figure out" God's plans:

> *My heart is not proud, LORD,*
> > *my eyes are not haughty;*
> *I do not concern myself with great matters*
> > *or things too wonderful for me.*
> *But I have calmed and quieted myself,*
> > *I am like a weaned child with its mother;*
> > *like a weaned child I am content.*
> > *Israel, put your hope in the LORD*
> > > *both now and forevermore.*

Even when we can't understand God's ways, we can trust His heart. And that trust—the surety of His unfailing love—brings us peace, rest, contentment.

As tempting as it may be to expend energy worrying about other people's burdens and baggage, comparing them to our own, let us choose to focus on ourselves. On what (and whom!) God has called *us* to bear. To forgive. To become. Just as Peter had to accept Jesus' plans for his life, so we have to accept His plans for ours. Broken and heartbroken as we may feel, comparison does us no good. It steals our contentment, distances us from God and others, and, in the end, changes nothing.

As we learned from Mary Magdalene, we can take comfort in knowing that God often calls us *because* of our weakness, *because* of our wounds, so that He can redeem them and use them for His glory. Different as we are, we each are called by God in different ways to different roles—but with the same level of devotion. Different, but the same. *"What is that to you? You must follow Me."*

No matter what specific roles, responsibilities, and even burdens God hands down to us, we each are called to give our all. To deny ourselves. To put Christ first, before our own desires, before any other relationship. To go with Him wherever He leads. Yes, on to victory, but also on to what the world would call "defeat." To unfairness. To crosses. To sacrifice. To wrongs that are not righted in this world. Even to death that only God will avenge.

Jesus Knows Your Thing

Jesus has a way of looking into our hearts, digging around, and uncovering the one thing that is keeping us from wholehearted devotion. He may not push that button at first, but eventually, He finds a way to push it. To call us to surrender that area of life to Him.

We see this clearly in His interaction with a wealthy young ruler who came to see Him. Jesus looked at him and loved him right away. Here was a likable, sincere guy with a desire to serve God. This young man had everything going for him—raised in faith, he knew the Law; he'd been faithful to God's commands, *and yet.*

As much as Jesus loved him, Jesus knew one thing stood in his way of total devotion: money.

> *"Teacher," he declared, "all these [commands] I have kept since I was a boy."*
>
> *Jesus looked at him and loved him. "One thing you lack," he said. "Go, sell everything you have and give to the poor, and you will have treasure in heaven. Then come, follow me."*
>
> *At this the man's face fell. He went away sad, because he had great wealth.*
>
> *Jesus looked around and said to his disciples, "How hard it is for the rich to enter the kingdom of God!"*
>
> MARK 10:20–23

I love the disciples' response to this exchange: the Bible tells us they were amazed (I suspect *flabbergasted* is probably a fair description!) and kept asking each other, "Who then can be saved?" In other words, "If this guy can't make it—this cool kid with his likable personality and solid family and big bank account—how in the world are *we* supposed to make it?"

Peter's response is my favorite. He says to Jesus, "We have left everything to follow you!" (verse 28). In other words, "Hey, Jesus, in case You hadn't noticed, we have already been super-disciples! We have given up everything—homes and families and jobs! Have You not noticed all of our sacrifices? And while I'm at it, what's in it for us?" *Classic.*

This time Jesus doesn't rebuke Peter for his comments; this time He encourages him with a generous promise: "Truly I tell you. . .no one who has left home or brothers or sisters or mother or father or children or fields for me and the gospel will fail to receive a hundred times as much in this present age: homes, brothers, sisters, mothers, children and fields—along with persecutions—and in the age to come eternal life" (verses 29–30).

Jesus didn't call everyone who wanted to follow Him to go sell everything first—it wasn't a universal command. But Jesus looked into this young man's heart and saw the one thing he was hanging on to. The one thing he loved more than Jesus. And sure enough, when Jesus called, the rich young ruler said no. He walked away sad.

If you keep finding yourself called to sacrifice the same thing, confronted by the same difficulty or weakness, perhaps, as with the rich ruler, Jesus is also looking at you and loving you, but gently saying, "This is your thing. The one thing I still need from you. Stop fighting it, and come follow Me. Yes, it will be hard, but watch Me repay you one hundredfold."

I spent several years trying my best to outrun conflict, particularly conflict in church. I had seen and experienced some hard things, and I thought, *Never again. You can have all of me, Lord, except this. The idealistic parts of my heart that people have trampled on.* And God in His kindness and patience let me hide and heal for a while. But then He put us on a mission team in a small church where everything is just *out there*—out in the open with a few people, and you just can't hide. He basically said, "Okay, Elizabeth, ready or not, it's time to grow." I have cried a lot, freaked out a lot, had more fist-shaking prayers than I care to admit, but I'm still here. Still growing. Still panicking my way through difficulties, still working through fear one clumsy conversation at a time. And you know, I think (I hope!) God is happy with that—happy with me. When He called, I didn't say, "Woo-hoo, I'm tickled pink about overcoming my fears, Lord! High fives all around!"—but neither did I walk away. Like Peter, I may be fumbling around, but I'm still here. I'm still growing.

Rising from Defeat

Few have fallen harder than Peter.

To deny Jesus not once but three times—the last time with Jesus watching, a deeply personal betrayal—what a deep shame; what a wound on the soul. How do you seek forgiveness from Jesus, then forgive *yourself* when you come to your senses? How do you find the confidence not just to walk with Jesus once more, once more to claim Him as your friend. . .but then to *lead other Christians* in faith and discipleship? Yes, few have fallen harder, but few have repented and recovered so dramatically! As much as Peter said no in the courtyard, he spent the rest of his life saying yes.

Just weeks later, Peter finds the courage to preach the first Gospel sermon, ushering more than three thousand thirsty souls into God's church in one day (Acts 2). And then a few weeks later comes this moment: the same Peter who so recently cowered in the dark before a servant girl now stands unashamed before the entire Jewish Sanhedrin (the same leaders who had pushed for Jesus' death).

> *Then Peter, filled with the Holy Spirit, said. . .*
> *"Know this, you and all the people of Israel: It is by*
> *the name of Jesus Christ of Nazareth, whom you*
> *crucified but whom God raised from the dead, that*
> *this man stands before you healed. Jesus is*
> *" 'the stone you builders rejected,*
> *which has become the cornerstone.'*
> *"Salvation is found in no one else, for there is no*
> *other name under heaven given to mankind by which*
> *we must be saved."*
> *When they saw the courage of Peter and John*
> *and realized that they were unschooled, ordinary*
> *men, they were astonished and they took note that*
> *these men had been with Jesus.*
> ACTS 4:8, 10–13

What boldness! What repentance! What transformation! In spite of the dangers, Peter found the confidence and courage to stay in Jerusalem shepherding and leading a fledgling church. What a way to bounce back. To rise to a new challenge—a changed role— after a painful defeat.

One day, many years later, someone did take Peter to that place he didn't want to go. Church tradition holds that Peter was executed for his faith, crucified upside down because he didn't consider himself worthy to die the same death as his Lord. Yes, Peter went where he did not want to go.

But the moment the last breath left his body, we can be sure he heard the smiling voice of his old friend saying, "I told you I would get your room ready. Welcome home—come on in."

Peter gives me hope: hope for myself, hope for all of us. Let us learn from Peter that even when we fail—say no, break faith, run away—all is not lost. We have not blown our one and only chance. God can still use us. We can still serve, still lead others *to* Christ and *in* Christ.

Peter proves that when we say no—even the worst kind of no—Jesus is willing to give us another chance. A chance to change. A chance to turn our no into yes. A chance to turn our "But Lord, I—" into "But God can." A chance to go wherever He leads, whenever He calls.

Jesus called Peter to go not once, but many times. So with us: "Go and tell. . . . Go and make disciples. . . ." And just as with Peter, so our Lord doesn't only send us out; He also brings us in. Invites us close. For every *go*, there is also a *come*: *Come and see, go and tell. Come and heal, go and share.* Always, our faith goes both ways:

> *"Come. . .and you will see."*
>
> JOHN 1:39

> *"Come, follow me, and I will show you how to fish for people!"*
>
> MARK 1:17 NLT

> *"Come to me, all you who are weary and burdened, and I will give you rest."*
>
> MATTHEW 11:28

Come see, come follow, come rest. Jesus doesn't only send us out on our own; He also calls us to Himself: Walk with Me, watch Me, know Me. Follow Me, learn from Me, be like Me. *Come near. Come now. Come stay.*

And when we come to Jesus, when we answer His call—"Tell me to come to you on the water." . . . *"Come!"*—He walks before us and beside us. Even fishes us out of the water when we flounder.

When we come to Jesus, we get to share His joy:

> *"Come and share your master's happiness!"*
>
> MATTHEW 25:23

> *"Come, you who are blessed by my Father; take your inheritance, the kingdom prepared for you since the creation of the world."*
>
> MATTHEW 25:34

Like Peter, let us be brave enough to jump up onto the prow of the boat, lean out over the waves, and shout, "Lord, if it's You, tell me to come."

Then Jesus will turn, flash a proud smile, hold out a hand, and call, "Come!" *Come conquer your fears. Come share My adventure. Come walk with Me.*

And when Jesus says, "Come," there's only one way to respond: we cast fear aside, let go of the rope, and jump overboard, shouting, "I'm coming, Lord! Let's go!"

> *Let the one who hears say, "Come!" Let the one who is thirsty come; and let the one who wishes take the free gift of the water of life.*
>
> REVELATION 22:17

> *Then Jesus came to them and said, "All authority in heaven and on earth has been given to me. Therefore go and make*

disciples of all nations, baptizing them in the name of the
Father and of the Son and of the Holy Spirit, and teach-
ing them to obey everything I have commanded you. And
surely I am with you always, to the very end of the age."

MATTHEW 28:18–20

Let's Go Deeper. . .

For Further Study
You can read some of Peter's later victory stories in Acts 2; 4; 5:17–42; 12:1–19.

Journal Prompt
1. What spiritual struggle keeps cropping up in your life?
2. If Jesus were to call you to change one thing today, what would it be?
3. In what areas is it tempting to compare your burdens with others'? How can you make peace with your burdens, your past, and your current role?
4. In what areas do you think God is most proud of you?

Prayer Prompt
Create in me a pure heart, O God,
*   and renew a steadfast spirit within me.*
Do not cast me from your presence
*   or take your Holy Spirit from me.*
Restore to me the joy of your salvation
*   and grant me a willing spirit, to sustain me.*
Then I will teach transgressors your ways,
*   so that sinners will turn back to you.*

PSALM 51:10–13

Notes

Chapter 6

1. If you suspect that you are experiencing true depression, I hope you will find the courage it takes to talk about it. The courage to continue tackling your thoughts and feelings with scripture and prayer, but also to set up an appointment to be professionally evaluated. If you are diagnosed with an emotional issue that requires treatment, I hope you will embrace the help.

Chapter 7

1. Mary had at least six other children—Jesus' half siblings—several of whom are named in scripture: James, Joseph, Simon, Judas, and unnamed "sisters," meaning that Mary had at least two daughters (see Matthew 13:55–56).

2. We assume Joseph died, since he does not appear in scripture after the story in Luke 2:41–52, and since Jesus makes arrangements for his mother's care after Jesus' death (see John 19:26–27).

Chapter 8

1. Haddon W. Robinson, *Decision-Making by the Book* (Grand Rapids: Discovery House, 1998), 49.

2. Lara Casey, *Make It Happen* (Nashville: Thomas Nelson, 2014), 162.

3. Os Guinness, *The Call* (Nashville: Thomas Nelson, 1998), 51.

Chapter 9

1. This list of diagnostic questions is adapted from a sermon my father (Sam Laing, WarriorfortheLord.com) has often given to help other Christians identify their giftedness. As always, Dad, thanks for so generously using *your* spiritual gifts to help the rest of us find ours!

Chapter 11

1. To be clear, we do not know from scripture if Nabal was an abusive husband; the Bible depicts cruelty, stinginess, arrogance, drunkenness, and folly. How that translated into his relationship with Abigail we can only guess. This passage is not intended as a text to guide our decisions in whether to stay in a difficult or abusive marriage—a topic outside the scope of this book; this story is meant to show Abigail's courage and wisdom, and to recount an important development in David's life.

About the Author

Elizabeth Laing Thompson is also the author of *When God Says, "Wait."* She writes at LizzyLife.com about clinging to Christ in the chaos of daily life. As a minister, speaker, and novelist, she loves finding humor in holiness and hope in heartache. She lives in North Carolina with her preacher husband and four miracle kids. They were totally worth the wait, and they always keep her on the go.

If You Liked This Book,
You'll Also Like...

Elizabeth Laing Thompson

When God
Says
wait

Navigating life's *detours and delays*
without losing your faith,
your friends, or your mind

When God Says, "Wait" by Elizabeth Laing Thompson
Author Elizabeth Laing Thompson invites readers to walk alongside
people of the Bible who had to wait on God. . .like David, Joseph,
Miriam, and Naomi. Their stories will equip us to live our own
stories—particularly our problematic waiting times—with faith,
patience, perspective, and a healthy dose of humor.
Paperback / 978-1-68322-012-1 / $14.99

"When God Says, 'Wait' is a must-read. Elizabeth gives us confidence
and courage in times of waiting, ensuring that we
will be better because of the wait."
–Lara Casey Isaacson, author of *Make It Happen*

Elizabeth Thompson is a kindred spirit. I love her writing style, heart,
and quirky humor. She writes with authenticity and wisdom.
–Andy Lee, author of *A Mary Like Me: Flawed Yet Called*